THE ROBBER BARONS AND THE SHERMAN ANTITRUST ACT

MILESTONES
IN AMERICAN HISTORY

ALEXANDER GRAHAM BELL
AND THE TELEPHONE

THE ATTACK ON PEARL HARBOR

THE CALIFORNIA GOLD RUSH

THE CIVIL RIGHTS ACT OF 1964

THE ELECTRIC LIGHT

THE LOUISIANA PURCHASE

THE MONROE DOCTRINE

THE OUTBREAK OF THE CIVIL WAR

THE PROHIBITION ERA

THE ROBBER BARONS AND
THE SHERMAN ANTITRUST ACT

THE SINKING OF THE USS *MAINE*

SPUTNIK/EXPLORER I

THE STOCK MARKET CRASH OF 1929

THE TRANSCONTINENTAL RAILROAD

THE TREATY OF PARIS

THE WRIGHT BROTHERS

THE ROBBER BARONS AND THE SHERMAN ANTITRUST ACT

RESHAPING AMERICAN BUSINESS

TIM MCNEESE

CHELSEA HOUSE
PUBLISHERS
An imprint of Infobase Publishing

The Robber Barons and the Sherman Antitrust Act

Chelsea House
An imprint of Infobase Publishing
132 West 31st Street
New York, NY 10001

Library of Congress Cataloging-in-Publication Data

McNeese, Tim.
  The robber barons and the Sherman Anti-trust Act : reshaping American business /
Tim McNeese.
    p. cm. — (Milestones in American history)
  Includes bibliographical references and index.
  ISBN 978-1-60413-008-9 (hbk.)
  1. Trusts, Industrial—United States—History. 2. Big business—Moral and ethical
aspects—United States—History. 3. Industrialists—United States—History. 4. Antitrust
law—United States—History. 5. United States. Sherman Act. I. Title. II. Series.
  HD2795.M425 2009
  338.8'20973—dc22   2008025317

Text design by Erik Lindstrom
Cover design by Ben Peterson

Printed in the United States of America

Bang NMSG 10 9 8 7 6 5 4 3 2 1

This book is printed on acid-free paper.

CONTENTS

1 Introduction   **1**

2 A Colonial Economy   **12**

3 A New Economic Century   **23**

4 Technology and Industry   **38**

5 The Robber Barons   **48**

6 Antitrust Gains Popularity   **65**

7 The Sherman Antitrust Act   **77**

8 Antitrust in the New Century   **91**

Chronology and Timeline   **106**

Notes   **111**

Bibliography   **113**

Further Reading   **115**

Index   **118**

Introduction

Outside the University Club of New York, the night was cold. It was December 12, 1900. Inside the elite, Fifth Avenue club were about 80 of the wealthiest, most influential American businessmen, financiers, and industrialists, who collectively represented an estimated $5 billion of investments. They had gathered, seated at long banquet tables, to honor the president of the largest industrial foundry in America, Pittsburgh's Carnegie Steel. Thirty-seven-year-old Charles Schwab was a mover and shaker in the high stakes world of American business, but he had not always been in such a position. He had joined the ranks of the great industrialists through hard work, starting at the bottom, as a dollar-a-day stake driver for Andrew Carnegie, the son of a Scottish immigrant, who had made it big in America in the steel business. Now, he was the dynamic young man who worked for Carnegie as the operating president of Carnegie Steel. Life had been good to Charles Schwab.

A WESTERNER BY REPUTATION

During the meal, which included the usual seven- or eight-course fare to which these tycoons were accustomed, there was little conversation, and much of that was restrained. Nearly all of those gathered did not really know Schwab other than by reputation. He was a "westerner" to them—someone who did business out in the wiles of western Pennsylvania. Now Schwab, who had staked out a place in the booming business world of the new American century, whose career had blossomed along the banks of the Monongahela River, would be familiar to them. Charles M. Schwab would no longer be just a name—he would become a force to reckon with.

Among those gathered at the University Club banquet and seated directly at Schwab's right was another American tycoon, a Wall Street financier, maker of American railroads, and organizer of such important corporate entities as General Electric, American Telephone & Telegraph, and International Harvester. Twenty-five years Schwab's senior, J. Pierpont Morgan fit the part of a powerful, turn-of-the-century American multimillionaire. He wore the requisite three-piece suit, with a gold watch chain. He sported a great walrus mustache and a thinning crown of white hair. His eyes were deep-set and piercing. Most prominent among his facial features was his great, bulbous nose, a reddish strawberry appendage with which he suffered a maddening skin condition called rosacea acne. All that mattered little. Morgan did not command people by his physical presence. He commanded them with the power of his corporate will. He could bring a corporation into existence with a nod of his head, plus the $100 million he might raise as investment capital. No one steered the ship of American industry in 1900 as did J. Pierpont Morgan.

Charles M. Schwab (left), shown here with Edward N. Hurley (right) in 1918, was the president of both the Carnegie Steel Corporation and Bethlehem Steel. It was a speech by Schwab in 1900 that prompted J.P. Morgan to make his bid to buy Carnegie Steel, paving the way for the formation of United States Steel.

Morgan had been seated next to Schwab for a reason. It would be easier for him to hear Schwab's speech when the time came following the dinner. Schwab's message was intended for every man in the room, but especially for Morgan. When the president of Carnegie Steel rose that evening, he spoke about "a bright future of low prices and stability for the steel industry."[1] He went on to explain his plan to retool his company into a scientifically integrated firm, a move that he believed would revamp the entire industry. Through this "vertical integration," Schwab explained, all the elements of steel production would be owned by the steel company. All phases of production (the mining of iron ore and coal, the shipment of the raw materials to the steel plants, the manufacture of the steel, and the transport of the finished steel products) would be owned by Carnegie. There would be no middle man: no awkward system of production dependent on a host of outside companies, each responsible for its piece of the steel-producing puzzle. Carnegie would own the mines, the ships, the mills. There would be no need for competition. The steel industry of the future, Schwab assured his audience, would lie in the hands of an immense steel conglomerate, a monster corporation that would command the industry, one built on the scrap heap of other steel companies and steel products producers. As Morgan listened, he certainly heard Schwab's message. He was well aware of the events from earlier that year that now prompted the steel president's speech.

CARNEGIE AND STEEL

In previous years, Carnegie Steel had only produced raw steel, leaving the manufacture of the more refined steel-based products to other companies. Through those same years, J. Pierpont Morgan, as a financier of corporate powers, had been working hard to create trusts for those companies that produced such finished steel items as tubes and wire. Trusts were a relatively new form of business corporation. A trust brought together the previously competing producers of a given product, uniting them into a single company with a common board of directors. The whole point of such trusts was to put immediate competitors out of business. The steel products trusts had not proven effective, due to one hitch. That hitch was Andrew Carnegie. Carnegie, as the country's largest producer of raw steel, did not like trusts.

When American Tin Plate Company, a steel products firm that bought raw steel from Carnegie, approached Carnegie and threatened to stop doing business with his company unless he refused to sell steel to American Tin Plate's competitors, the wealthy Scottish American was outraged. Rather than give in to such pressure, Carnegie decided to do battle. He joined several informal arrangements called "pools," which were business agreements between competing producers to fix their prices. With Carnegie unbowed by the steel products trusts, Morgan and his associates realized they had a problem in Andrew Carnegie. Their plans to draw together in trust and control their corner of the steel industry would not work if Carnegie did not cooperate with them. In July 1900, less than six months before the banquet at the University Club of New York, Morgan and his business allies in National Tube, American Steel and Wire, and American Hoop decided to cancel all their contracts with Carnegie Steel. The new plan was a bold one: to drive the biggest steel producer in America out of business. Morgan and his steel-producing associates planned to either buy their steel from other companies or produce it themselves in their own steel plants.

Carnegie was not a man to go down without a fight, however. He had no intention of backing down from Morgan or anyone else. Once he learned of Morgan's plan, Carnegie telegraphed his company's officers, including Charles Schwab: "Crisis has arrived, only one policy open; start at once hoop, wire,

One of the nineteenth century's most powerful financiers, John Pierpont Morgan (pictured here in 1881) was instrumental in assembling the huge trusts that came to dominate American business in the early 1900s. Building on a family inheritance, Morgan was quick to sense the profit potential in almost any situation; he successfully speculated in gold, rifles, and railroads.

nail mills . . . Extend coal and coke roads, announce these; also tubes. . . . Have no fear as to result, victory certain. Spend freely for finishing mills, railroads, boat lines."[2] Carnegie was matching fire with fire. He would spend money to create his own steel products companies and cut out his competition that was threatening to cut him out. Schwab immediately took the reins. He informed his boss that they could produce steel tubes at $10 less per ton than National Tube. That summer, Schwab chose not to pay any dividends to stockholders in Carnegie Steel. He would begin construction on a $12 million tube plant, instead.

With the threat of Carnegie-owned steel products companies looming, the affected manufacturers scurried that fall to J. Pierpont Morgan for assurance and advice. They were panicked. The president of Federal Steel, Elbert Gary, put their fears into words, stating that Carnegie could "have driven entirely out of business every steel company in the United States."[3] With the crisis still looming, the invitation to the University Club dinner reached Morgan. He would take the bait. He would go to the dinner in honor of his nemesis's right-hand man, Charles Schwab, and listen to what he might have to say.

A MEETING ON MADISON AVENUE

The speech not only informed Morgan, it appears to have inspired him as well. He went back to his home at 219 Madison Avenue and spent the following week digesting Schwab's message and its implications. As for Schwab, he returned to Pittsburgh to his duties as president of Carnegie Steel. Eventually, Morgan contacted Schwab, suggesting that they meet to talk. Schwab did not jump at the offer from the Wall Street tycoon, explaining he was uncertain that his boss, Mr. Carnegie, would like his steel company president meeting privately with Morgan. By January, he agreed, however, to meet Morgan at the Bellevue Hotel in Philadelphia. When Morgan fell ill and, unable to make the trip, remained at his home in New York, Schwab made the trip to him.

On the night of January 5–6, 1901, Schwab met with Morgan in the great, mahogany-paneled library of his Madison Avenue manor house. Along with Morgan and Schwab, two other men were present that evening in Morgan's "black library." John Warne Gates was the controller of the American Steel and Wire Company, an entrepreneur who had started out as a barbed wire salesman in San Antonio. The fourth party present was one of Morgan's partners, Robert Bacon, a handsome young man known for his athleticism, whom Morgan referred to as "the Greek God."[4] The Wall Street tycoon peppered Schwab with questions by the dozen: What companies would be included in a new steel supercorporation and which ones would be left out? Would Carnegie consider selling his steel company? If so, what would be his terms? What would be his price? Their talks went on through the night. The steel president came to the meeting prepared. He had brought along six sheets of figures and the statistics of several companies. With these, he explained their worth and their potential earning capacity. When the sun rose on a new day, January 6, Morgan gave instructions to Schwab: "Well, if Andy wants to sell, I'll buy. Go find his price."[5]

Schwab went and did just that. He found the steel magnate on the frost-covered links of St. Andrews in Westchester, playing a wintry round of golf, the Scotsman bundled up in sweaters. The Pittsburgh-based steel president knew not to talk business on the course, and he waited until Carnegie finished his game. Only after the two men had sat down to enjoy the fireside warmth of Carnegie's nearby cottage, did they finally get down to business. Schwab informed his boss of the all-night meeting with Carnegie's nemesis, J. Pierpont Morgan, and told him that Morgan wanted to buy him out. Carnegie listened with keen interest. He was tired of the business world and had been considering retirement. He was 65 years old. He might even go back to Scotland where he owned a grand castle.

Carnegie told his steel president to give him a day to consider selling out and at what price.

The following day, Schwab met with Carnegie again. This time, the steel tycoon handed him a slip of paper on which he had scrawled the magic number, his selling price for Carnegie Steel. Schwab then met with Morgan, handing him the paper. Morgan opened it and looked at the number Carnegie had written out in pencil: $492,556,000. It was a staggering sum, more than "double Carnegie's own valuation a few months previously."[6] Most people, even modern businessmen, would have been awestruck by the enormous figure. Few people in the country ever thought in terms of money any greater than a million. Morgan was looking at a figure approaching a half *billion* dollars. His answer to Schwab was short and brusque, one he offered without flinching: "I accept."[7] The greatest financial transaction in history to that date had just been made, informally, through a glance at a slip of paper and a verbal agreement through a third party. A few days later, Morgan called on Carnegie at his office. The two business tycoons faced one another and shook hands, further sealing the deal. As they grasped hands, Morgan said to Carnegie, almost matter-of-factly, "Mr. Carnegie, I want to congratulate you on being the richest man in the world."[8]

A DRAMA MADE OF STEEL

Like latter-day gladiators, these businessmen of the new century had locked in combat and emerged having negotiated an agreement of epic proportions. Carnegie retired, moved to Scotland, and gave over the rest of his life to philanthropy, giving away countless millions of his titanic personal wealth to the endowing of libraries, as well as anything else he wanted to support. Morgan went on to create the supercorporation that Schwab had dreamed about that cold winter's evening in December 1900. In the days following the agreement, Morgan

Now known chiefly for his philanthropy, Andrew Carnegie (pictured here in 1913) built one of the nineteenth century's largest fortunes by investing in steel production, which was essential for the rapid growth of railroads and manufacturing in the United States.

formed his giant corporation, which he called United States Steel. He capitalized his venture with $1.4 billion. U.S. Steel would control more than 50 percent of the steel produced in the United States.

The drama between Carnegie and Morgan did not end there. A year later, the two financial titans met on a transatlantic voyage aboard an ocean liner. Standing on the ship's deck, Carnegie expressed his singular regret concerning the sale of his steel business to Morgan: "I made one mistake, Pierpont," explained Carnegie. "I should have asked you for $100 million more than I did." In a sense, Morgan then had the last laugh. Turning to Carnegie, he said, "Well, you would have got it if you had."[9]

During the last decades of the nineteenth century through the early twentieth, business tycoons such as J. Pierpont Morgan and Andrew Carnegie ruled the American industrial landscape like lions on the Serengeti. They brokered deals, and accumulated companies and profits as regularly as they drew breaths. It was a time of giant profits and sometimes unscrupulous business combinations, such as pooling arrangements and trusts meant to discourage competition. There seemed to be no end to the rapacious appetites for gain and corporate power among the nation's financial leaders, those whom some referred to as the "robber barons." How far would they go in their quests for control of America's industrial base? Would there be no end to their profits? Would the federal government continue to turn a blind eye to the share-taking of a handful of the country's rich and powerful? Would the American economy remain a playground for the rich or would a day come when an angry nation, tired of paying the corporate pipers, would finally say enough is enough?

A Colonial Economy

When Jamestown, Virginia (the first permanent English colony in North America), was established in 1607, its destiny was not certain. Indeed, the colony of only 100 men and boys almost died out altogether. These early colonists were barely able to scratch out an existence in the New World, much less establish a vibrant economy. Growth did take place, however, not just in Jamestown and Virginia, but in the other 12 English colonies established between 1607 and the 1730s. Throughout that lengthy period of colonial settlement and expansion, the colonists were able to survive only after establishing an economy that could support them by providing food, their livelihoods, and enough surplus food and manufacture to sell for a profit. For many colonists, their earliest significant trade was with local Native Americans, who provided food in exchange for metal hatchets, iron kettles, and a myriad of beads and other trinkets.

SIMPLE COLONIAL ECONOMIES

Throughout the American colonial period, the colonies established regional economies typically centered on tapping the land's natural resources to produce farm products. Through the decades of the 1600s, colonial farmers grew fields of grain such as wheat, barley, and rye; tobacco, which proved to be a profitable cash crop for many Southerners; as well as other crops, including corn, rice, and indigo. Much of the agricultural production of the southern colonies was done by black slaves imported from Africa. Trees grew in abundance in the colonies, so viable lumber industries flourished. Fishing and whaling were major industries. By 1700, "New England had a fleet of 2,000 shipping and fishing vessels, virtually all of local manufacture."[1] Shipbuilding became a mainstay for several northern colonies, especially in New England's Massachusetts, Rhode Island, and Connecticut.

The colonies did not develop any significant industrial base until the last half of the 1700s. In the meantime, many colonial residents were skilled craftsmen, those often referred to as the "leather apron men," who produced a wide variety of practical goods needed in the colonies, including barrels, boots, soap, ale, guns, rope, silver service, canvas for ship sails, and a host of others. American shopkeepers printed newspapers, repaired shoes, baked bread, fashioned hats, pounded horseshoes, dipped candles, and shaped pottery. Much of what these skilled artisans produced were "bespoke" goods, goods that had been "spoken for" or ordered by consumers and then made.

Between the mid-eighteenth century and the beginning of the American Revolutionary War in 1775, the American economy expanded even more. From its colonial ports, a tidal wave of exports set sail for destinations that included Europe

This print depicts the 1607 landing at Jamestown. Called "James City" by its English settlers, Jamestown was settled under the auspices of the Virginia Company of London on James Island, a deep-water anchorage 60 miles up the James River from where it empties into Chesapeake Bay.

(including England), Africa, and the Caribbean with daily regularity. Everything from rice to tobacco to indigo to tall, straight pine trees intended for ship masts were traded out to points abroad. Much of the colonial output was agricultural or in natural resources such as lumber, but a small manufacturing sector was developing. By the beginning of the American Revolutionary War, the Chesapeake Bay region was noted for its flour mills, which used the latest equipment. Distilleries in Philadelphia produced more than 200,000 gallons of rum annually, much of it intended for export. With local iron deposits available in many colonies, there were "more forges and furnaces than [in] all of England and Wales and exceeded them in the output of pig and bar iron."[2]

Helping to stimulate a growing economy was a growing population, which provided a greater workforce and expanded markets for domestically produced products, as well as trade goods imported from overseas. In 1630, the English colonies in existence at that time were home to approximately 5,000 colonists. At the beginning of the American Revolutionary War in 1775, 2.5 million people called America home. Not only was the overall population developing, but colonial cities were growing as well. Philadelphia was "the second largest city in the English-speaking world by 1776, with 35,000 inhabitants."[3]

Throughout most of the colonial era, taxes in America were low. The average tax might run near 5 percent. By the second half of the eighteenth century, however, New York and Boston had established tax rates as high as 10 percent. In Philadelphia, they had increased even more. When the British Crown attempted in the 1760s to place new and higher customs taxes on trade goods to the colonies (especially manufactured goods from Great Britain and commodity goods such as coffee and tea) Americans refused to pay them. This rejection ultimately led to the outbreak of the Revolutionary War and a break from British control. The United States of America was established as a free and independent nation.

CHANGING DIRECTIONS

By the late 1780s, the new United States changed political direction. The limited confederacy of states that had been created under the nation's first constitution, the Articles of Confederation, had failed miserably. The Articles government had included only a single-house legislature, no president or executive leader, and no national court system. The Articles had been constructed to maximize the power of each individual state while creating a weak national government. That government had been unable to even regulate trade between the states, a situation that fostered economic chaos. In the summer of 1787, delegates to a constitutional convention held in Philadelphia chose to scrap the poorly constructed Articles in favor of a new constitution that created a federal system in which power was shifted from the states to the national government. The new constitution created a viable executive branch, embodied in a president, as well as a judiciary system that included a Supreme Court and several lower courts.

George Washington, the Revolutionary War general, took the office of president in the spring of 1789 and soon appointed approximately 125 men to government jobs, including justices of the Supreme Court. He also chose fewer than a half dozen advisors for important cabinet positions. Among those handpicked advisors was a 34-year-old New Yorker who had served General Washington as an aide-de-camp during the war. Alexander Hamilton was appointed as the nation's first secretary of the treasury, one of the most important appointments Washington made to the small federal government. It fell to Hamilton to take control of the major financial problems gripping the national government. Washington's administration inherited a $54 million debt, including interest. In addition, the states owed another $25 million. As he sought solutions to the debt problem, Hamilton realized he had before him the opportunity to develop a financial program that would mirror his own political beliefs.

Hamilton advocated a powerful federal government. As an intense nationalist, he wanted the new republic to have as solid a financial footing as possible. In 1790, he wrote his *Report on the Public Credit*, in which he expressed the importance of eliminating the debt and establishing good credit for the federal government. He went so far as to suggest that the national government assume the debts of the states by borrowing new monies at a lower interest rate. After a six-month debate, Hamilton finally got his proposal through Congress. (To gain southern support for his plan, he agreed to have the federal capital

Alexander Hamilton (1751–1804) was the first secretary of the treasury. During his tenure, Hamilton controlled postwar debt and prevented the country from sliding into bankruptcy.

moved farther south, along the banks of the Potomac River, not far from George Washington's home at Mount Vernon.)

Another Hamilton proposal called for the creation of the Bank of the United States, which he patterned after the Bank of England. The bank's purpose would be to issue money to the federal government and to private borrowers. Although the new constitution said nothing about a national bank, Hamilton claimed the bank could be created under the "implied powers" clause of the constitution. The Bank of the United States would become reality under a 20-year charter, beginning in 1791.

Hamilton made yet another economic proposal during his early years as secretary of the treasury. In December 1791, he submitted another paper, his *Report on Manufactures*, perhaps his most far-reaching proposal. In it, Hamilton made clear how much he was a supporter of private enterprise. He expressed his belief that a successful American republic would have to invest in supporting manufacturing and the building of factories and systems of domestic industry. He thought it important that the American economy be diverse so that the American people would not be dependent on the importation of foreign goods. Included in his reports was a call for higher tariffs on foreign imports that would make American-produced goods competitive and protect American industry; limits on the exportation of important raw materials out of the country; financial incentives to encourage would-be American manufacturers; rewards to American inventors; embargoes to keep American production techniques from leaking out to other countries; and the formation of a national board to support agriculture and new manufacturing.

Hamilton's broad-based program foresaw an America in which the country would become more industrialized, its cities would become larger, and the nation would become less rural. He could not have predicted better. Yet, at the time, most of his proposals concerning the national encouragement of manufacturing fell on deaf congressional ears. Although Congress did pass new tariffs, they chose to ignore Hamilton regarding expanding nonfarming, domestic production. As a result, the United States continued to remain dependent on Europe's manufactures, which were paid for through exports of American farm products.

DIFFICULTIES FOR THE ECONOMY

Perhaps in the early 1790s, the future was difficult for most Americans to envision. The new republic was only a few years old, nearly everyone worked in farming, and the country's cities were fairly small. In fact in 1790, only two American cities, New York and Philadelphia, boasted populations greater than 25,000 residents. Nevertheless, the U.S. economic growth that Hamilton predicted began to take place before the end of the eighteenth century, even if the growth was somewhat slow. Throughout the decade, the number of banks increased tenfold. Exports more than tripled from $29 million to $107 million. Close to a dozen factories and mechanized mills were built during the decade. Economic growth was happening, just as Hamilton had hoped and planned.

By remaining dependent on European manufactured goods, the new republic found itself vulnerable even before the start of the next century. When war broke out between Great Britain and France during the 1790s, American merchants and shippers tried to remain neutral and trade with both sides. Such European conflicts, however, led to both powers systematically seizing American ships on the high seas and searching them for cargoes bound to their enemies' ports. Between 1805 and 1811, British and French naval vessels and privateers captured hundreds of American merchant ships. There was no American navy to stop such actions.

Thomas Jefferson, who served as president between 1801 and 1809, could not simply sit by while ship seizures continued. In February 1806, he requested Congress to pass the Non-importation Act, which prohibited the importation from Great Britain of a lengthy list of items including cloth and metal articles. The act was designed to pressure the British by boycotting imports. Although the act was in effect through much of 1806, it was replaced in 1807 by a tougher act known as the Embargo Act. This act closed American ports to all foreign trade in an attempt to put international pressure on Great Britain and France.

The act was a disaster for the American economy. Thirty thousand sailors lost their jobs. Some desperate American seamen joined the British merchant marine for employment. Exports fell 80 percent from $108 million in 1807 to $22 million in 1808, with devastating results. Ships rotted in their docks, while grass grew up along American wharves. Unemployment shot up. Ironically, the embargo did not seem to immediately hurt Great Britain. The Embargo Act did so much damage to the American economy in just two years that President Jefferson finally withdrew the embargo just before the end of his second term. The act was replaced later in 1809 with another restrictive trade law, the Nonintercourse Act. This new legislation reopened all foreign trade with the United States except for Great Britain and France. The act also empowered the new president, James Madison, to reestablish trade with either nation once that nation had ended its practice of violating America's neutral rights. The international interference with American trade, the embargo, and the closing of American ports, among other events, led down the same road. The economy of the new republic took serious hits, and recovery would take several years of rebuilding and retooling America's production systems and reestablishing its overseas markets.

REBUILDING AFTER THE WAR

The young American republic emerged from the challenges of the War of 1812 with a renewed sense of its own economic and industrial future. During the two decades following the war, the United States experienced important changes in transportation, technology, and productivity on its far-flung farms and plantations. The country experienced extensive urbanization as many people in rural areas moved to the country's towns and cities, even as European immigrants arrived by the shipload, with many making their homes among their former countrymen and women from the Old Country. By the 1830s and 1840s, America had made great strides, transforming itself from a largely rural country into one of the most industrialized nations in the world.

It is crucial to understand, in the midst of all this great economic upheaval, just how rural and agricultural the United States was at the beginning of the 1800s. In the oldest settled regions of the country (the North and the South), between 90 and 95 percent of the people lived on farms, on plantations, or in hamlets and villages no larger than 2,500 residents. The population of the United States was small, only numbering approximately 5.3 million people. (By comparison, Great Britain's population numbered 15 million and France's stood at nearly twice that, 27 million.) The American population was spread out over a great expanse of territory amounting to hundreds of thousands of square miles.

Across this broad republican landscape, many people lived remotely, rarely venturing out of their part of the country, perhaps never straying more than 50 miles (80.5 kilometers) from home. Those who traveled found it slow and difficult. An early nineteenth-century stagecoach ride over the 189 miles (305 kilometers) between Boston and New York took three days; the ride between New York and Philadelphia took two. In the South, travel was even more difficult. There was no public transportation system of any kind, with the exception of a stagecoach line running between Charleston and Savannah. Moving people around was typically slow, but the mail service was even slower. In 1800, it took nearly three weeks to mail a letter from Maine to Georgia.

America at the turn of the nineteenth century was still a fairly primitive place. Many people lived in frontier houses and log cabins. Farms were underdeveloped pieces of real estate. Farmers still used primitive plows, did not rely on fertilizers, and rarely fenced in their livestock. Farm life for many at the outset of the new century was little different than it had been at the start of the eighteenth or even seventeenth centuries.

As for anything remotely resembling a factory or manufacturing system, the United States had little to show for itself. Most people produced nearly everything they needed for their daily lives; they would, however, buy a few manufactured goods if they found them on the shelves of a local store. At home, Americans were their own manufacturers, producing their own clothing, blankets, candles, soap, tableware, and even tools. The largest industries in the country (iron-making, textiles, and clothes-making) were generally small production systems. Together these three vital industries at the turn of the century employed only about 15,000 workers.

At the opening of the United States' first full century, the new republic's economy seemed backward, nearly stagnant, and certainly unimpressive—especially to industrialists in Great Britain, which by then was deeply invested in the Industrial Revolution, with its steam engines and early factory system. Great American innovations lay just ahead. From the days of the War of 1812 through the presidency of Andrew Jackson in the 1830s, the United States was second only to Great Britain as the greatest industrialized power in the world.

A New Economic Century

When the new American century opened in 1800, reliable and inexpensive transportation for people and goods was nonexistent. Roads were poor and inadequate, little better than they had been during the colonial period. English-style stagecoaches, with their egg-shaped bodies, were the primary type of travel for passengers from one city or state to another. Due in part to the poor conditions of roads, stagecoaches were slow, jolting, and uncomfortable. When loaded with passengers, luggage, and additional freight, the early nineteenth-century stagecoach might hit a top speed of 4 miles (6.4 kilometers) per hour.

NEW MEANS OF TRANSPORTATION

Some new-and-improved transportation systems were introduced to the American landscape during the early decades of the 1800s, such as the 66-mile-(106.2-kilometer-)long Lancaster Pike, a stage and wagon road connecting Philadelphia and Lancaster, Pennsylvania, or the National Road, built with federal dollars, that began in Maryland and eventually reached St. Louis. The country also experienced a dramatic canal-building boom that resulted in the construction of more than 100 major canals. During the 1820s and 1830s, more than $125 million was spent on building these man-made waterways of commerce and passenger service.

Even though canals might have solved the transportation problems of many of the country's regions, they were not the answer for everyone or every place. Such cities as Boston and Baltimore, where canals were not practical, began to develop some of the nation's earliest railroads. After experimenting with British locomotives, which were often too heavy for American rail lines and bridges, the first American locomotive was built in 1830. These early models became part of the Baltimore and Ohio Railroad, as well as the Charleston and Hamburg Railroad. In New York, despite the existence of the Erie Canal, the Mohawk and Hudson Railroad was built.

These early railroads in America were short, dangerous, and unreliable. The original rails were made of wood, not iron or steel, and were kept in place with metal straps nailed to the rail ties. The boilers on steam locomotives exploded so frequently that early trains included barriers of cotton bales to protect passengers. Open rail cars were swamped with black smoke from the engine and sparks landed on passengers regularly. One female traveler from England once found 13 burn holes on her dress following a ride on a short American rail line. Despite these initial problems, technology slowly improved, and railroads were soon under construction across the country all the way to the Mississippi River and beyond. During the 1830s alone, railroad companies built more than 3,300 miles (5,323 kilometers) of rail track, surpassing the number of miles of canals built in America by that time. By modern standards, these early trains were slow, poking along at 10 miles (16 kilometers)

This locomotive, called the Locomotion, was designed and built by George Stephenson for the Stockton and Darlington Railway in 1825. Located in England, it was the world's first public railway powered by steam.

per hour. This was, however, more than twice the speed of the era's stagecoaches, canal boats, and even steamboats. Once again, a new transportation system of the early nineteenth century helped to lower the cost of delivering raw materials to the country's mills, foundries, and factories, as well as finished goods to the consumer. Toward mid-century, railroads helped link America's East and West.

Railroad development brought innovation to American transportation at the same time that a new technology began revolutionizing communication by the 1840s. Even by the 1830s, communication and transportation had already improved dramatically. Reporting the death of George Washington in 1799 had required a week's travel between Virginia and New York City. In 1831, President Jackson's State of the Union address reached New York from Washington, D.C., by fast stagecoach in just under 11 hours, due largely to improved roads. The real sea change in delivering information took place when inventor Samuel F.B. Morse electrified communications with his telegraph, which came on line in 1844. The telegraph created instant communication across long distances.

RESISTANCE GIVES WAY TO THE FUTURE

New technologies such as steamboats, railroads, and the telegraph were destined to change America dramatically during the first 50 years of the nineteenth century; nevertheless, the introduction of such technologies often created controversy. When the century opened, many Americans were skeptical of such innovations. Some workers believed that new transportation and factory systems might threaten their jobs by making them obsolete. The result was that the United States was slow to take on these new ways of doing things. Although practical steam engines were invented in Great Britain years before 1750, there may have been only one working steam engine in the entire United States as late as 1800. The year 1790 introduced the first American textile mill. Even 10 years later, only eight such mills were in operation in the states.

The nation's new surge of inventiveness was not always received enthusiastically, which held back potential progress. The early steamboat designer and inventor, John Fitch, never gained enough enthusiasm for his boat projects and failed. Similarly, Oliver Evans's plans for an American locomotive during the 1780s and 1790s never succeeded. Unable to gain financial backing, he died in 1819 dreaming of trains that would be built a generation later. Early nineteenth century America was so driven by agriculture that there were few mechanics who even knew how to build such things as steam engines or mechanical devices for factories. When steamboat inventor Robert Fulton needed an engine for his new boat design in 1807, he had to purchase one from England. No one in America knew how to build one.

By the 1820s, however, America's general skepticism about mechanical devices, steam engines, and other new contraptions had been largely overcome. Through the work of hundreds of inventors, amateur mechanics, tinkerers, and metalsmiths, concepts for new inventions and mechanical devices became working, practical models. People were beginning to see the value of such machines, noting how they could provide better transportation, better communication, and better productivity. A French visitor to the United States during the 1820s noted America's new craze for machinery: "Everything new is quickly introduced here. There is no clinging to old ways; the moment an American hears the word 'invention' he pricks up his ears."[1]

AMERICA'S EARLY FACTORIES

As the United States became more driven by mechanics and inventors during the 1820s and 1830s, the country began seriously developing its manufacturing sector. After all, creating a working invention in a workshop was one thing; having a place to produce such devices in large numbers was another. What drove this new interest in manufacturing in America was the desire to produce goods in quantity to help lower their costs. The country soon became so immersed in developing new factory systems that Europeans referred to these new techniques of manufacturing as the "American System."

Factories were not entirely new to America, even in the years following the War of 1812. During the 1790s, an English mechanic and immigrant to the United States, Samuel Slater, built one of the country's earliest factories, patterned after production plants in Great Britain. (Slater had helped design such facilities before coming to America.) His mill was constructed in Pawtucket, Rhode Island, to produce textiles. Other factories that opened during the 1790s produced iron, brass, paper, glass, firearms, nails, even umbrellas. Generally, these were small facilities. In addition, the decade witnessed the establishment of the country's first blast furnace west of the Allegheny Mountains of Pennsylvania, a hallmark of the iron and steel

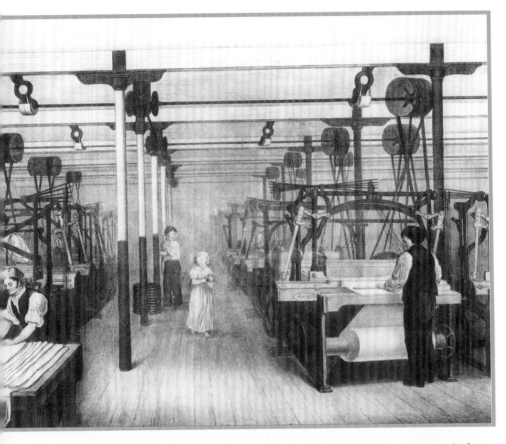

This print shows a textile factory in the northeastern United States during the nineteenth century. The textile industry was one of the first to move to the factory system.

industry that would dominate in western Pennsylvania during the nineteenth century.

These early plants laid the groundwork for America's factory system; by the 1820s and 1830s, the system was teeming with innovations. A couple were the applications of mass production and the standardization of product. The greatest innovator of American mass production was a northerner named Eli Whitney. Today, he is remembered for his 1793 invention of the cotton gin, a simple tabletop device that cleaned the sticky seeds from cotton lint, helping to make Southern cotton production more viable. Whitney became convinced that the secret to factory productivity was to mass produce items by making all their component parts identical. He first applied this idea to the manufacturing of firearms. In 1798, Whitney convinced U.S. government officials to offer him a contract to manufacture 10,000 muskets within two years. At the time, his offer seemed absurd. The American arsenal in Springfield, Massachusetts, was only producing 250 muskets in two years. Whitney's plan was to construct a factory in which machinery would be installed that was designed to produce precision-made gun parts that would be interchangeable; a lock mechanism, for example, would be so finely made by machine that it could be used on any musket.

To see his plan through, Whitney first had to design and build drill presses, lathes, cutters, and metal grinders that would allow even an unskilled factory worker to produce precision parts, work that had previously been done by skilled gunsmiths. Whitney received his contract, and although he did not succeed in producing in two years as many guns as he had promised, the concept of interchangeable parts had become reality. Soon, other industries were adopting this aspect of the American System. By the turn of the century, plants had been built that mass-produced clocks and other domestic goods. Over the following decades, everything from sewing machines to farm equipment was being mass produced using interchangeable parts. This drive for factory precision gave significant rise to the machine tool industry, those plants that produced the machines such as lathes and cutting tools that were used in factories to mass produce other goods.

Everywhere, industry was changing America. Many Americans, naturally, remained farmers, but industry changed the ways they farmed. In the 1790s, a New Jersey farmer named Charles Newbold invested $30,000 of his own money in designing a cast-iron plow. (Unfortunately, it did not sell well. Many farmers believed the iron would contaminate the ground and encourage weed growth.) Twenty years later, a New Yorker from Scipio, Jethro Wood, patented his own iron plow using interchangeable parts. Such devices were laborsaving. Old-style wooden plows required two men and two pair of oxen to plow a single acre of land in a day. Wood's new plow required only one farmer and one pair of oxen to accomplish the same work.

SLATER AND HIS AMERICAN MILL

They were willing to pay. In 1789, the Pennsylvania legislature ran an advertisement in newspapers in England offering money to any English textile mill worker to immigrate to the United States and bring along his knowledge of English mill designs. America had no such mills, and no one in the country had the skill, knowledge, and experience to operate such a mill.

In Derbyshire, England, an interested mill worker read the American ad. Samuel Slater immediately left Derbyshire, went to London, and took passage on a ship to the United States, landing in Philadelphia. He had not been able to leave England easily. Offers similar to that made by the Pennsylvania legislators had become common in England, which boasted the best, most productive textile mills in the world. Skilled mill workers were not allowed to leave the country. Slater was forced to pose as an agricultural worker before English authorities granted him permission to leave England. He took his knowledge of building textile machinery with him.

When he arrived, he found work immediately. A Quaker merchant, Moses Brown, had only recently completed construction on a textile mill in Pawtucket, Rhode Island. Brown had big plans for his mill, but he had no one with the experience to operate it.

By 1830, America was on the path of becoming an industrialized country. Factories, mills, and foundries were springing
up, especially across the Northeast. In 1807, American cotton
mills numbered between 15 and 20, operating approximately
8,000 thread spindles. Less than a generation later, the mills
in operation had dramatically increased so that the number
of spindles stood at approximately a quarter million. Steam

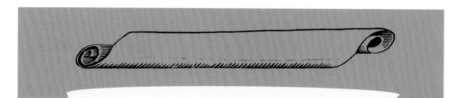

Fortunately, the newly arrived Slater applied for the needed position.
Brown hired him, even though Slater's price was high. The English
mechanic was to take all the immediate profits, after Brown sub-
tracted his costs of operating the mill and his interest on his investment. Days before Christmas of 1790, the mill went into operation.

It was a small operation, a mere matter of 72 spindles, each
spinning thread, all operated by seven boys and two girls between
the ages of 7 and 12. (At age 22, Slater was not much older than
his workers.) Slater worked the children hard, whipping them with a
leather strap when their work lagged. Soon, his young workers were
producing three times as much cloth as entire families of spinners
could produce at home. Profits were assured.

By 1793, Slater was partners with Brown and he set out to construct a mill of his own. Five years later, Slater built another mill
separate from Brown, in a partnership with his brother John. The
factory was called the White Mill. Through the first three decades of
the nineteenth century, Slater continued to build more mills. In all,
he would own all or part of 13 textile plants. By his death in 1835,
Slater may have been a millionaire. The 1793 Slater Mill still exists
today and serves as a museum dedicated to Slater's contribution to
early American manufacturing.

engines were used in every industry. By 1830, mechanics in the city of Pittsburgh, a frontier town at the turn of the century, were producing 100 steam engines annually. Many items that traditionally had been made at home were now being produced in the country's factories and mills.

CHANGES IN AMERICA'S BUSINESS LAWS

With the expansion and development of a progressive American economy increasingly based on manufacturing, changes were soon needed for the country's business laws. At the turn of the nineteenth century, the American legal system still revolved around an agricultural society. The law "presumed that goods and services had a just price, independent of supply and demand."[2] There were laws that the courts used to limit some types of competition as well as innovation. The court system actually protected monopolies. For example, when Robert Fulton built his steamboat in 1807 and successfully demonstrated it on the Hudson River, he gained a monopoly on the use of steamboats on the Hudson from the New York State legislature. Such exclusive rights were commonplace in the early nineteenth century. Early nineteenth-century laws strictly protected landowners. A farmer might be allowed to sue a mill owner if his mill caused a river to flood the farmer's property. Following the War of 1812, American law began to change, moving in favor of economic growth and industrial development. Courts began to side increasingly with manufacturers, viewing profit and corporate risk as beneficial for the country as a whole.

The American legal system changed in other ways. By the 1820s, American laws sought to catch up with the new reality of a country driven by a market economy. Especially in the Northeast, where industrialization was concentrated, new laws came on the books that allowed for a greater competitive market. The courts were also recognizing the legitimacy of the economic law of supply and demand. Previously, the law was based on the assumption that goods and services had "an objective price, independent of supply and demand."[3] Old usury laws, which limited interest rates, were eliminated and replaced with laws that assumed that the market would set the appropriate interest rates, as well as prices. All this provided the foundation for a truer form of American capitalism.

Everything was about economic growth. The courts, along with many state legislatures, handed greater privileges and powers to the country's privately held companies and manufacturers. Construction companies that contracted to build the nation's new roads, bridges, canals, and even railroads later were granted new powers of eminent domain, which allowed them to appropriate land from private owners on behalf of the public good. The courts reduced the level of liability a company might have for injuries on the job, requiring, instead, for the injured employee to prove he or she had not been negligent in causing his or her own injury. Companies were also able to bypass penalties for causing fires, floods, or even loud noise levels produced by factories or other production plants. For America's early manufacturers, the legal system was definitely tilted in their favor.

As the country's economic and business laws changed, the U.S. Supreme Court typically made decisions that supported an expanding economy. Under the leadership of Supreme Court Chief Justice John Marshall, the Court issued several key decisions during the years following the War of 1812. In 1819, the Court decided an important case that pushed for bankruptcy laws to become more uniform from state to state. In another decision, *Dartmouth College v. Woodward*, the Court sheltered corporations from interference from the government. One of the Court's most important decisions, *McCulloch v. Maryland*, established the constitutionality of the Bank of the United States and protected the national institution from taxation by the states. The 1824 case, *Gibbons v. Ogden*, limited the rights of states to hold back economic growth and competition by offering monopolies or bypassing laws that restricted trade.

THE AMERICAN SYSTEM

The drive to develop new American industry also had support from some of the nation's politicians. Following the War of 1812, the Federalist Party was dying, leaving political direction for the young republic in the hands of the Republican Party. (This party should not be confused with today's Republican Party, which was not established until the 1850s.) Among the

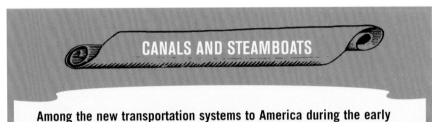

CANALS AND STEAMBOATS

Among the new transportation systems to America during the early 1800s was the construction of a multitude of man-made waterways called canals. Prior to the War of 1812, private companies, using state or private funds, carved out hundreds of miles of canals that crisscrossed the Northeast, connecting natural waterways such as lakes and rivers.

The longest was the Erie Canal, completed in 1825. The Erie stretched across upstate New York, from Albany to Buffalo, a total distance of 364 miles (587 kilometers). Add to these new waterways the invention of the practical steamboat, and river traffic in America took on a new dimension. The engineering required to build the canal's elaborate system of 84 locks, as well as 18 aqueducts, which sometimes allowed the canal to pass over preexisting rivers, was done without the benefit of modern engineering equipment. As one witness to the construction quipped, the Erie Canal was built "by guess and by God."* Such waterways had an immediate impact on the economy of the young republic. Prior to the canal, hauling one ton of freight from Buffalo to New York City cost $100 in wagon rates and took up to 20 days travel time. With the canal, the time dropped to less than a week as the price plummeted to $5.

Republican leaders were such brash, energetic congressmen as Henry Clay of Kentucky and John C. Calhoun of South Carolina. Both men urged their fellow congressmen and the president of the United States, James Monroe, newly elected in 1816, to throw their support behind anything that would build up the nation's economy. They campaigned for government backing of roads, canals, and a national banking system, as well as a

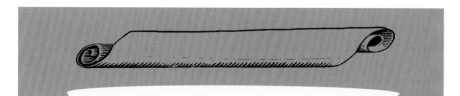

Even though canals dramatically altered the cost of shipping goods in America, other innovations were underway on America's rivers. For decades, a handful of American tinkerers worked their skills at designing and building a practical steamboat. Finally, New Yorker Robert Fulton demonstrated a workable boat that became a success on the Hudson River. Four years later, a steamboat was built in the Trans-Appalachian West, at Pittsburgh. The age of the steamboats moved ahead with lightning speed. A trip from Pittsburgh to New Orleans by flatboat, a distance of nearly 2,000 miles (3,225 kilometers), had previously taken as long as five or six weeks, with the boat traveling 24 hours a day. The new steamboats cut the time to a fraction. By 1817, the trip by steamboat from New Orleans to Louisville, Kentucky, had been reduced to 25 days. Two years later, newer models reduced the time to two weeks. Steam power was shrinking America's great western distances. A newspaper writer of the day summed the progress up: "If any one had said this was possible thirty years ago, we should have been ready to send him to a mad-house."**

---

*James Kirby Martin, America and Its People. New York: HarperCollins College Publishers, 1993, p. 276.
**Edward L. Ayers, et al., American Passages: A History of the United States. Belmont, Calif.: Thomson Higher Education, 2007, p. 265.

strong navy. The War of 1812 had proven to the Americans the value of a navy that could protect the nation's shipping interests, especially against Great Britain. The future of America, Calhoun and Clay claimed, lay in its commercial activities and its infant industries. Such positions would help establish the perimeters and goals of the American System.

Congressmen and President Monroe took up the challenges. Monroe encouraged Congress to pass legislation enacting strict protective tariffs in support of the nation's budding industries. He also campaigned for new federally funded road construction, especially for the western frontier. Such roads would connect regional markets and farming communities to one another. Monroe also pushed for canal construction, yet another transportation system that could further consolidate and connect America's markets.

One of the important needs for the early nineteenth century's ever-expanding economy was credit. Would-be manufacturers, businessmen, merchants, and others who wanted to establish new businesses or expand their existing operations needed capital to finance their efforts. Cash was in short supply, so credit was needed to provide capital. Prior to the War of 1812, the credit system in America was a joke, a poor system that was shaky, at best. For one thing, there were simply not enough banks and other lending institutions. Following the war, several states chartered new banks to help solve the cash shortage. By 1815, 200 new banks had been established, and, by 1818, nearly 400 new institutions were in operation. Such banks issued paper currency as bank notes to provide cash on a regional basis.

While hundreds of new state-chartered banks did help alleviate some of the cash and credit shortage in the country, they were not the final answer. Many such banks remained shaky themselves, issuing far too much paper money and offering credit too easily. Much of this credit was handed out to western land speculators hoping to make a quick profit. President

Monroe, along with many other influential leaders, threw his support to a new national bank to help bring stability to the national economy. The country had had a national bank earlier in its history, established in 1791 by Congress with a 20-year charter. Unfortunately, that charter had run out in 1811. Five years later, Congress voted to establish the Second Bank of the United States, based in Philadelphia. This bank was authorized to establish branch banks anywhere it wanted. Even though the bank was established by Congress, it was not strictly a government entity. Only one-fifth of the bank's directors were appointed by the government. The government used the bank to keep its federal deposits, but there were other, private investors. The national bank did serve the country well, working constantly to keep state banks on solid ground, control the money supply, and provide investment capital for new business ventures and manufacturing houses.

Technology
and Industry

The world of American business and industry changed dramatically during the remaining third of the nineteenth century that followed the American Civil War. That the nation's industrial sector expanded and grew is an understatement. The facts are clear: Despite the incredible amount of industry required to supply the fighting armies during the great American conflict in which nearly three million men fought, the United States emerged from the war with its industrial capacity still second-rate. From the end of the war until the turn of the century, however, the nation's manufacturing capacity became second to none. By 1900, American industry had reached a manufacturing output that exceeded that of the great industrial powerhouses of Europe (Great Britain, France, and Germany) combined.

It happened so quickly and to such an incredible extent. Growth multiplied in all sectors of the American economy from 1865 to 1900. The amount of land under cultivation in the United States doubled. The nation's gross domestic product (the value of all the nation's goods and services produced in a single year) grew to a level six times greater than what it was before the Civil War. The number of manufactured goods produced per person in the country tripled. Railroad mileage crisscrossing America increased from approximately 53,000 miles (85,483 kilometers) of track to nearly five times that number between 1870 and the opening of World War I. The country was linked east to west by rail during those years not just once, as in 1869, but five times. Even prior to 1890, track mileage had already reached 185,000 (298,387 kilometers). Along with this unparalleled railroad expansion came tremendous growth in American industry, which supplied everything needed to build railroads, including lumber, iron, and steel. Industrial development during these heady years of change was due to the groundwork laid by the industrial sector prior to the Civil War. Those were years of tapping the abundance of the land, of great breakthroughs in technology, and of a business world that gave its hearty support to industrial growth. The changes brought during the decades after the Civil War were sometimes so rapid that these new realities produced chaotic conditions, often in the form of conflict between the new workers of the 1870s, 1880s, and 1890s and the new business management styles of the owners of factories, mills, and mines having little or no direct interaction with those workers.

Modernization swept the country during the final third of the nineteenth century. Some of these progressive efforts brought about rapid change in the social order. Nearly every part of everyone's life in America experienced extraordinary change as phenomena such as electric lights, the telephone, the handheld camera, the typewriter, electric streetcars, and skyscrapers became reality. The workplace, the marketplace, and America's place among the great industrialized nations of the world would never be the same.

A BOUNTIFUL COUNTRY

The United States witnessed these great changes in industry and often benefited from them. Before immense quantities of manufactured goods could be produced in the nation's new factories and production plants, however, the raw materials for those finished goods, as well as the materials needed to power this period of tremendous economic growth had to be harvested. America had always been a land blessed with great stores of raw materials and natural resources, which the country tapped during the years following the Civil War as never before. Between 1850 and 1890, thousands of Americans worked in the nation's mining camps and corporate towns. Many desperately sought precious metals such as gold and silver during dozens of "rushes" scattered across the American West from California to Colorado to Nevada to the Black Hills of the Dakota Territory. In time, other natural resources were also mined to a greater extent, including copper, lead, zinc, quartz, oil, and even talc. These resources helped develop America's industrial base. In fact, many western mines were industrial centers on their own. Mining was an expensive business that required much investment, often through stock sales, and the purchase of heavy equipment. Many mining operations began through the efforts of individual prospectors and miners seeking their personal fortunes, but they became a matter of corporate investment on the part of wealthy Easterners seeking fortunes of their own.

The importance of utilizing the nation's mineral resources in the developing post–Civil War industrial base cannot be overemphasized. American industry prior to the Civil War had concentrated on the production of a handful of key commodities such as textiles, paper, and flour. The new industrial

America was about so much more. Industries were based on steel, petroleum, and the development of electrical power. There had been a viable iron industry before the war. Major iron deposits had been discovered during the 1850s in Michigan and Minnesota, and this iron was forged into plows and other farm equipment, but the durability of iron had always limited its use. The new industry would rework iron into a miracle metal—steel. At the center of that developing industry was a Scottish immigrant who had grown up in America. Andrew Carnegie and other steel men used a new technology to mass produce steel as never before. So innovative was their work that the age of steel was born. Its growth was phenomenal. In 1870, the country's foundries and mills produced 850,000 tons of steel. By 1900, steel production had mushroomed to 10.5 million tons and was growing.

This pattern was repeated during these decades with other natural resources. Copper had been used in the industry before the Civil War, but on an extremely limited basis. After rich copper discoveries were made in Butte, Montana, in 1881, copper could be mined in abundance, enough to become "a key ingredient in such new fields as oil refining, electrical generation and conduction, and telephone communications."[1] Again, the result was a growth metals industry. In 1860, the United States produced 8,000 tons of copper. By 1914, the tonnage produced was 100 times greater. Even by the turn of the century, the value of the copper being mined in the United States was greater than that of gold and silver combined.

Over and over, the numbers reveal the perimeters of the new American economy of the late nineteenth century. Coal production increased from a half million tons mined in 1860 to 270 million tons by 1900. The new industries relied on coal to provide much of their energy bases. Whereas earlier generations of Americans had relied on waterpower to run their mills and other facilities, by 1900, four out of every five factories and

This 1890s mining camp was in Ocean Grove, Colorado. The United States is rich in natural resources, and between 1850 and 1890, thousands of Americans worked in the nation's mining camps.

production plants relied on coal-burning steam engines for their energy. Some of these were replaced by oil and gasoline engines, especially with the arrival of the twentieth century.

Oil, in fact, became so much more important to industry than many Americans could have ever imagined. As early as the 1850s, oil fields in Pennsylvania had been discovered, typically forming pools of the gooey black stuff in natural springs and rivers. When it was tapped, much of this early oil was bottled and sold for its "medicinal" value. Before the decade was over, inventive men were drilling for oil and building oil wells, intending to use it for lighting lamps and as a lubricant for machinery. By the 1870s, 20 million barrels of oil were being produced each year. Early innovators, such as John D. Rockefeller, who became the greatest oil tycoon of the nineteenth century, turned the oil into kerosene for household lamps. Oil was well on its way to becoming one of the key linchpins of the burgeoning American industrial economy.

CHANGES IN TECHNOLOGY

The new American economy was driven by massive quantities of coal and, to a lesser extent, oil. These fuels needed something to fuel. The final 30 years of the nineteenth century delivered great changes in industry, in the machinery of the age, and in a raft of innovations that brought new technologies to the country. The number of inventions produced annually was growing rapidly. During the first 10 years after the establishment of the U.S. Patent Office in 1790, only 276 inventions were patented. A century later, in 1893 alone, patent office workers worked feverishly to register 22,000 new inventions.

These new inventions redefined life in America for many people. As one economist wrote in 1889: "What the world did not have half a century ago is almost equivalent to enumerating all those things which the world now regards as constituting the dividing lines between civilization and barbarism."[2]

Some of the greatest changes were introduced in the field of transportation. As railroads expanded their reach, the invention of the airbrake by George Westinghouse helped allow trains to become longer and faster. In America's cities, mass transit systems such as electric streetcars and electrified underground subway rails redefined the ways city dwellers moved through their urban jungles. Among the thousands of innovations were the typewriter, invented in 1867, and the practical adding machine, invented in 1888. With so many office jobs created during these years, such devices were immediate necessities. There were, for example, innovations in how newspapers were printed, and the pages of most newspapers were splashed with ads based on the new mass advertising techniques of the day. Photography, only having been invented during the years just before the Civil War, became a household phenomenon, with George Eastman's invention of the inexpensive, handheld camera in 1888. Few inventions of the last decades of the nineteenth century could rival the significance of Alexander Graham Bell's telephone, which transmitted the sound of the human voice for the first time publicly in 1876, during the nation's centennial celebration in Philadelphia.

INNOVATORS AND ENTREPRENEURS

Beyond Edison, other entrepreneurs worked to retool the American economic landscape. Some were not inventors themselves, but adapted existing innovations to develop new industries. One example was Gustavus Swift, a Chicago butcher during the 1870s who integrated an ice-cooled icehouse with an ice-cooled railway car to create America's first national meat-packing company by the mid-1880s. Some innovators completely retooled some industries, such as James Buchanan Duke who reinvented how cigarettes were made and packaged. He introduced a large cigarette-rolling machine in a company in which he was an investor. This massive one-ton piece of equipment was capable of producing 100,000 cigarettes in a day. At that time, the most skilled cigarette maker could only handroll 3,000 cigarettes daily. By utilizing new cigarette-rolling technologies, Duke was able to drop the price of cigarettes. When he redesigned the cigarette container as a crushproof sliding cardboard box, Americans were ready to take up cigarette smoking. (Most smoking prior to this invention involved pipes and cigars.)

A myriad of inventors each made their mark on the new technologies of the era, but none was as important as Thomas Alva Edison. He began his career as a candy peddler on local trains in New Jersey, became a telegrapher as a young man, and went on to become "the first great scientific inventor who clearly conceived of inventions as subordinate to commerce."[3] This was certainly how Edison saw himself, as he once noted:

> I do not regard myself as a pure scientist, as so many persons have insisted that I am. I do not search for the laws of nature, and have made no great discoveries of such laws. I do not

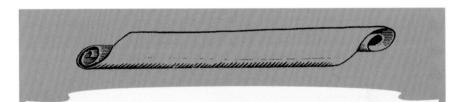

By 1890, Duke had bought up four tobacco companies, introducing new production techniques in each, and then formed them into one business—the American Tobacco Company.

The new drive in American industry, then, relied, in part, on scientist-inventor businessmen. Most American businessmen of the decades following the Civil War were not great innovators or inventors. They were simply ordinary businessmen who operated small production plants or factories or wholesale stores. Even though they may have been "ordinary," theirs were not typically rags-to-riches stories. Most of the business leaders of the period came from backgrounds of relative wealth. The vast majority were born in the United States, not abroad. Nine out of ten were raised either in middle class or upper class homes. Approximately one of every three was a college graduate. About 50 percent did not start out young, as enterprising and hard working boys, but began their working careers at age 19 or older. Only 25 percent or so began working prior to the age of 16.

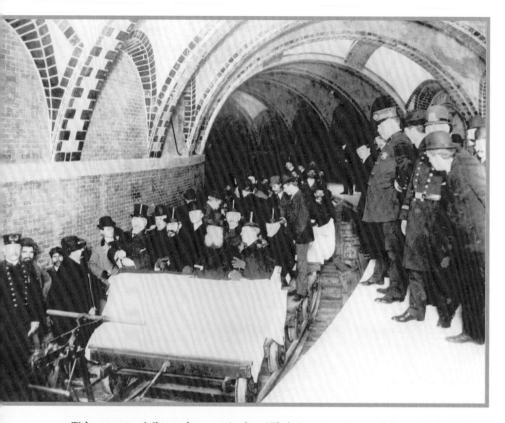

This group of financiers and city officials get a tour of New York City's first subway in January 1904 while the city's policemen stand by on the platform at City Hall Station. Innovations in railway design allowed the first underground railroads to be built in the late nineteenth and early twentieth centuries.

study science as Newton and Faraday and Henry studied it, simply for the purpose of learning truth. I am only a professional inventor. My studies and experiments have been conducted entirely with the object of inventing that which will have commercial utility.[4]

He established a research laboratory in Menlo Park, New Jersey, in 1876, where he held court over a small army of tinkerers, mechanics, and electricians. It was there that Edison promised "a minor invention every ten days and a big thing every six months or so."[5] It would prove to be a promise he nearly kept. Some of his greatest inventions helped thrust the nation's reliance on technology to a new level, including the phonograph in 1877 and the incandescent light bulb two years later. He either invented or developed better working models of the telephone, the Dictaphone, the mimeograph, the dynamo, motion pictures, and electrical transmission. To that end, he founded the nation's first electric company in 1882 in New York City, an effort backed with money from one of the nation's richest businessmen, J. Pierpont Morgan. Six years later, Edison established General Electric Company to mass produce light bulbs.

AMERICA'S NEW ENTREPRENEURS

As seen in Edison's example, new technologies and new inventions helped to create new businesses. Following the Civil War, new businesses were established by the thousands. By 1870, the United States was home to approximately a half million business firms. (The country's hundreds of thousands of farms are not included in that number.) Many of those businesses were small operations employing a handful of workers, but some were giant corporations whose workers numbered in the thousands. By 1870, America's workforce numbered a staggering 13 million. Of that number, approximately 2.5 million were working in manufacturing jobs. Among those manufacturers, the 10 biggest industries, in order from most important, were flour and other grain products, cotton goods, lumber, boots and shoes, men's clothing, iron, leather, woolen goods, liquor, and machinery. The lumber industry, which employed the most people, had only 160,000 workers, which was much smaller by far than the employment within the largest industries in America today.

The Robber Barons

In addition to the inventors, innovators, and ordinary businessmen who contributed to the new American business and industrial base, another type of business leader emerged during the years following the Civil War. Even though they remained small in number, they came "to dominate and drive and dazzle their fellow businessmen. By virtue of their personalities, their ambitions, their talents, . . . their tactics, these business leaders bestrode the economic landscape like Gullivers in the land of Lilliput, endowing the age with many of their personal characteristics."[1]

Their business methods gained them a label, a name that compared them to the medieval lords of the feudal world, rulers who dominated the economy, mistreated their workers, and made those who challenged them and their power pay dearly. They were the men known as the "robber barons." Among their number, a few extraordinary men stood out for their ruthless business behaviors. One of the most notorious was a railroad tycoon from Pennsylvania named Jay Gould.

WALL STREET MEPHISTOPHELES

To some, Jay Gould was not just a brilliant and ruthless businessman; he was "the Mephistopheles of Wall Street."[2] He was driven by money, financial power, and the accumulation of assets, perhaps more so than any man of his time. Nothing could deter him from his cold-steel efforts to gain, no matter who else might have to lose. He appears to have been heartless, having no natural human controls that often guide others. As one historian described him with his eyes wide open: "No human instinct of justice or patriotism caused him to deceive himself, or to waver in any perceptible degree from the steadfast pursuit of strategic power and liquid assets."[3]

He began his public career in 1856, at the age of 20, as a partner in a leather tanning factory in Pennsylvania. Gould quietly took up embezzlement, "investing" the factory's profits in real estate gambles. When his crime was uncovered, he formed a partnership with new investors in the tanning operation and continued to embezzle company funds, driving one of his ruined partners to suicide. By the time Gould was finally driven out of the tanning business in 1861, he had accumulated a small fortune from the firm's profits.

Gould soon moved on to another capital venture. Throughout the 1860s, he invested in railroads. He became one of three board members for the Erie Railway in 1867. His fellow board members were cut from the same cloth as Gould. Jim Fisk was known for his intense desires to accumulate profits, and Daniel Drew had made some of his early profits through "watered stock," the practice of denying cattle water until just before selling them and then bloating them with water to add weight at the sale.

An archetypical example of a robber baron, Jay Gould acquired a railroad empire, a newspaper, and the Western Union Telegraph Company. Frequently criticized by the press for his ruthless business tactics and for his consolidation of financial and political power, Jay Gould was considered the most hated man in America at the end of his life.

A year after forming their railway triumvirate, Drew, Gould, and Fisk were soon vying against a would-be takeover. One of the richest men in America, "Commodore" Cornelius Vanderbilt, who had accumulated a fortune in the shipping industry, had taken up buying railroads during the Civil War. His eye fell on the Erie Railway. He soon became enmeshed in a scheme cooked up by the three Erie investors, who issued $8 million in overvalued stock ("watered stock," to use the cattle analogy) in the company. When a New York court issued an order restraining the sale of the overpriced stock, Gould and company spent $1 million bribing New York legislators to pass a special law allowing the stock transaction. Gould's tactics even frightened Drew and Vanderbilt, who recalled the stock issue and chose to divest themselves of the Erie, leaving it to Gould and Fisk. Undeterred, the two remaining board members issued almost three times as much bloated stock as they had originally planned.

Such business tactics as stock watering and outright bribery were not limited to unscrupulous business tycoons such as Jay Gould. The era following the Civil War was a ruthless business age known for its deceitful, illegal, and unethical practices. Even Thomas Edison offered a few thousand dollars each to New Jersey legislators who supported bills that served his interests. Stock watering was rampant. Vanderbilt, although choosing to separate himself from Gould and the Erie Railway, nevertheless watered stock. When he gained controlling interest in the New York Central Railroad, at the time one of the nation's most important, he increased the company's stock value by an arbitrary $23 million, nearly all of which went into his pocket. When confronted on the illegality of the move, Vanderbilt is alleged to have stated: "Law! What do I care about the Law? Hain't I got the power?"[4]

Such unscrupulous activities on the part of the era's business movers and shakers would not have been possible without

THE STATUE UNVEILED.

In this satirical cartoon, the "statue" is railroad giant Cornelius Vanderbilt, who in 1869 tried unsuccessfully to assume control of James Fisk's
Erie Railway by buying out its stock. Here he stands, like the Colossus
of Rhodes, at the crossroads of the New York Central and the Hudson
River railroads, both of which he owned. A steamship in the background
symbolizes his commercial shipping interests. At left a diminutive Fisk
waters his own line, the Erie, using a bucket and hand-powered pump
while eyeing his competitor enviously.

the cooperation of government. Throughout much of the nineteenth century, the prevailing economic philosophy in America
was that government should maintain, in general, a hands-off
approach to the economy and not attempt to control economic
activity with restrictive laws. The economic concept was known
as "laissez-faire," a policy that assumed that government's role
was to simply let the country's economy run according to
natural, economic laws. This concept was first espoused in the
publication of *The Wealth of Nations* in 1776 by an economic
thinker named Adam Smith. Smith argued that a free market

economy was led and controlled by an "invisible hand," one composed of several individual economic choices made by those participating in a given economy, including producers and consumers. If government intrusion is kept to a minimum, a competitive, free economy will experience positive growth by producing the needed goods for that market at reasonable prices. At the heart of his economic philosophy was the idea of supply and demand, an economic law that assumes that a product in short supply and high demand will experience a price increase, whereas overproduction of a good, relative to demand, will cause the price to drop.

GOVERNMENT LENDS AN ECONOMIC HAND

Typically, neither the federal government nor the state governments tried to impact the country's economy through significant manipulation, but that is not to say that the government did not help the economy in certain ways. Government not only aided big business through tariffs, it also handed out land grants to businesses such as railroads. Businesses could also benefit from legislation that favored industry over labor. Legislation provided businesses with low-interest loans. For a time, such laws were not unpopular with the American public. Many Americans believed these laws helped to expand the national economy, which they interpreted as a good trend for themselves and the country. Industrialization was sometimes seen as a patriotic effort by big businessmen. Oil tycoon John D. Rockefeller was thinking in those terms when he justified his business activities: "I wanted to participate in the work of making our country great."[5] Only later in the century, when the abuses perpetuated by unscrupulous business leaders became obvious, did the nation as a whole begin to decry the robber barons.

The government, then, lent its support to the American economy and to big business through tariffs, land grants, and low interest loans and by not passing restrictive legislation. With the way clearly paved for economic expansionism during the late decades of the nineteenth century, business leaders increasingly turned to consolidating their places in the American economy. Those who wanted to command the economy from the greatest heights knew they could not do so by remaining small or by relying on businesses that were individually owned or kept in the hands of limited partnerships. This gave rise to the number and scope of American corporations.

Corporations were not new to America during the late 1800s. The first permanent, English colony in North America, Jamestown, was established in 1607 by investors in a joint-stock corporation. Other colonies were also built on the efforts of English-based corporations. The value of such business entities was to share not only the profits of an investment but also the

GOVERNMENT AND PROTECTIVE TARIFFS

During most of the nineteenth century, the American economy operated on a laissez-faire basis. Government intrusion, manipulation, or control of the economy was almost nonexistent—just how the great industrialists wanted things. Prior to 1887, there were no national regulating agencies meant to control any part of big business.

The economy of this period in American history, however, was not entirely free of government involvement. From the founding of the United States, the federal government had enacted tariffs on foreign imports, a system that protected domestic industry and its products. The policy of tariffs had been controversial from time to time, but few Americans sought an end to protective tariffs during the nineteenth century. Many tariff rates only increased as the century moved on.

Congress and various presidents saw to that. At the end of his presidential term, President James Buchanan (1857–1861) signed risks. For example, investors purchase stock and assume a level of risk that rises with their number of stock shares. Corporations also provide a means of hedging one's investment bets. One could buy a 10 percent stock share in 10 railroads rather than invest entirely in one railroad.

Even though corporations stretched back to the beginning of seventeenth-century settlement in America, changes in how corporations were formed took place during the first half of the nineteenth century. Some of these dated to the 1830s when Andrew Jackson was president. The first significant corporation change was a shift from having states issue charters for each corporation to exist. Newer laws allowed a business, individual, or group to incorporate without state permission,

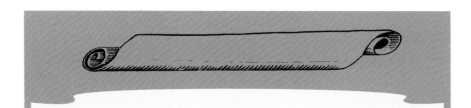

the Morrill Tariff, which raised tariff rates for the first time in nearly 20 years. That increase immediately set the stage for tariff rates to continue to increase throughout the remainder of the nineteenth century and into the twentieth. Initially during the post–Civil War era, such tariffs on certain American-made products made some economic sense. The budding steel industry needed tariff protection against European competition. Even after the American steel producers, such as the great steel tycoon Andrew Carnegie, had managed to plant themselves firmly in the steel market and even lower the price of steel by reorganizing production techniques, the tariff on steel remained in place. One of the results of these unnecessary tariffs was to produce greater profits for steel producers at the expense of consumers paying higher prices. While the average tariff rate in America stood at 50 percent, some tariff rates were as high as 80 percent.

assuming the laws were satisfied otherwise. After the Civil War, the business concept of "limited liability" was upheld by the courts, where, under earlier laws, bankruptcy might result in not only the loss of one's business but also one's personal assets. Under new laws, a corporation's liability ended when all assets were lost. One such court decision was *Santa Clara County v. The Southern Pacific Railroad.*

This decision was probably based on a distortion of the scope of the U.S. Constitution's Fourteenth Amendment which guarantees "equal protection of the law" as well as "due process" of the law. The decision ruled that a corporation should be defined as a legal "person" protected by the amendment. In other words, a law governing a corporation also had to apply to all individuals. Corporations, therefore, had the "right" to acceptable profits, which the courts, not the states, would decide on. The decision was a perversion of the Fourteenth Amendment. In actuality, the *Santa Clara* ruling gave special privileges to corporations, rather than providing "equal protection." Corporate "persons" were rarely punished for crimes committed in the name of a corporation. A popular quote of the day stated "that a corporation had neither a soul to be damned nor a body to be kicked."[6] The result was a great increase in the number of American corporations. By 1904, 70 percent of all industrial plants were operated as corporations.

With the American economy rapidly expanding during the final three decades of the nineteenth century, there was plenty of investment capital for new corporations. The law favored corporations, states placed few restrictions on them, and investors were, at least in part, protected. The years following the Civil War and into the early twentieth century were extremely favorable toward corporations. It is not surprising that they became such dominant economic institutions and that the country's industrial sector grew so quickly. In effect, through much of the 1880s, few wanted to stop the proliferation of corporate America and the industrialization it supported. The words used by an attorney for John D. Rockefeller rang true: "You might as well endeavor to stay the formation of clouds, the falling of rains, the flowing of streams, as to attempt . . . to prevent the organization of industry."[7]

KEEPING COMPETITION TO A MINIMUM

It was not the existence of so many corporations in America that lay at the heart of the controversies that later surrounded them. It was that the corporations dominated the national economy through their sheer size and through the fact that many were based on a lack of competition. During the second half of the nineteenth century, many American business leaders did not actually advocate free enterprise based on competition in the marketplace. Competition only kept profits low. As one American envelope manufacturer put it: "Competition is industrial war. . . . Unrestricted competition, carried to its logical conclusion, means death to some of the combatants and injury for all. Even the victor does not soon recover from the wounds received in combat."[8] Some businessmen made it their mission to eliminate free competition. They were searching for order in the American economy, as was Wall Street tycoon J.P. Morgan, who thought that "the American economy should ideally be like a company organizational chart, with each part in its proper place, and the lines of authority clearly designated. He did not really believe in the free enterprise system, and like most ardent socialists, he hated the waste, duplication, and clutter of unrestrained competition."[9]

Railroads were the first big business in America to systematically try to eliminate competition. These transportation systems required a tremendous amount of capital, resulting in mountains of debt for most lines. When too many railroads serviced the same region or cities (for several years following the Civil War there were 20 railroads competing for the rail services between St. Louis and Atlanta), competition cut deeply into profits. In an attempt to lure business from competitors, railroad owners gave rebates to large freight customers over long distances while overcharging small haulers, such as individual farmers. These shady tactics, of course, did not ultimately make railroads more profitable. In time, railroads servicing the same customers created cooperative systems called "pooling arrangements" through which the lines would divide up potential customers and raise their rates, since the arrangements cut back on competition.

In one sense, such arrangements were nothing new on the American economic scene. Dating back to the colonial period, those who produced similar goods often agreed not to undercut one another. Their business maxim was "live and let live." To that end, colonial business, as well as many businesses prior to the Civil War, agreed to set the same prices for identical goods, thus eliminating one aspect of competition. These new pooling arrangements went even further, to the point of nearly cutting out all competition. By the 1880s, pooling agreements were common. There were many railroad pools: a salt pool, a whiskey pool, and a coal pool, among others. Such arrangements did not sit well with customers or even the government. They were eventually made illegal under a congressional act passed in 1887 called the Interstate Commerce Act.

Ultimately, the most successful answer to the railroads' problems with competition was accomplished through consolidation. How multiple rail lines were sometimes combined into fewer or even a single line with no competition involved ruthless business tactics. In 1867, "Commodore" Cornelius Vanderbilt eliminated his direct competition by this method. To become the controlling interest in the New York Central Railroad (NYCR), Vanderbilt bought up two competing rail lines that connected with the NYCR. Then, he placed a ban on all rail cars going to or from the New York Central. His plan worked, but he was harshly criticized for eliminating competition. His response was nearly indignant: "Can't I do what I want with my own?"[10] The Commodore proceeded to purchase additional railroads connecting to the NYCR between New York and Chicago, and then expanded to other cities. The result was just what he had planned: an integrated railroad system that was efficient and profitable, and one that was owned by him, with the profits going to him, with no significant competitors. Other railroad magnates would pursue the same tactic with their railroads, ultimately resulting in a drop in the number of competing rail systems between the 1870s and 1890s.

ROCKEFELLER'S NEW TACTIC

Even though consolidation offered significant advantages to big business, another business organizational practice came into general use following the Civil War. Oil entrepreneur John D. Rockefeller would be among the first to develop this business tactic in America. Just as a glut of individual and competing railroads cut deeply into profits and created a chaotic economic landscape for the transportation system, so competition was making it difficult for the oil industry. Because drilling costs for a well were typically low, many would-be oil men got into the business, creating small companies that inevitably had to compete with one another. In Rockefeller's words, "the butcher, the baker, and the candlestick maker began to refine oil."[11] With a plethora of wells and oil companies in America, the price of oil typically fluctuated wildly. To a businessman like Rockefeller, the oil industry needed stability.

John D. Rockefeller was born in 1839 in the town of Richford, New York. After working and investing in the grain and meat businesses in Cleveland, he turned to a new industry. Rockefeller entered the oil business as a small competitor himself during the Civil War, in 1862. Achieving his own success, he founded the Standard Oil Company of Ohio in 1870, a large corporation established with an initial capital outlay of $41 million, a tremendous amount of money at that time. His approach to business was cold and calculating:

Those who worked with him could not help but admire his decisiveness, his sureness of touch, and his infinite resourcefulness. Rockefeller knew how to fasten upon and make the most of the opportunities that were presented to him. When his inner clock told him that the time was ripe, he was capable of acting with a speed, an authority, and . . . a ruthlessness that never failed to impress his subordinates.

Rockefeller was a deadly competitor. He forced railroads to give him rebates on his huge oil shipments. He sold below cost in particular communities to steal business from local refiners. Then he gave the refiners a choice: Sell out to Standard Oil or face destruction.[12]

Rockefeller worked hard to keep competition with his oil company to a minimum. Eventually, he tried something new: He created a trust. Under the then-existing corporation laws, such a business practice was perfectly legal. In a trust, the stockholders in a corporation hand over their stock to a centralized board of directors to hold "in trust," in exchange for trust certificates. The directors are then empowered to vote the stock as they see fit. Company profits continue to be paid to the shareholders as they had before this special arrangement was made.

Rockefeller's goal was to combine as many oil refineries in the United States as possible into one large refining company, eliminating nearly all competition and streamlining the industry into a well-oiled, corporate machine. The man he hired to put all that oil business under the same umbrella was Samuel C.T. Dodd, Standard Oil's top attorney. In 1882, Dodd organized the Standard Oil Company trust, a structure designed to establish a board of directors responsible for overseeing 40 corporations, all from offices set up in Standard Oil's New York City headquarters.

The new corporate structure was seen as an immediate success, both by Rockefeller and then by other corporate leaders across the country, and trusts proliferated quickly. Soon, there was a sugar trust, a cottonseed oil trust, and a host of others. Even before the end of the decade, "trusts were a well-nigh ubiquitous feature of industry."[13] There were so many trusts that, as one clever newspaper writer noted, "an average citizen was born to the profit of the milk trust and died to the profit of the coffin trust."[14]

Along the way, the concept of the trust was tweaked and refined. One variation was the "voting trust," which further managed to sidestep competition in the marketplace. This business technique was also known as the corporate merger, by which one corporation bought up a majority of the stock in another corporation, thus further consolidating production of a given commodity under one, larger corporate roof. Before the innovation could go into general practice, corporate laws had to be altered, since it was not lawful for a corporation to own stock in another corporation or company. New Jersey would lead the way, amending its incorporation laws to allow corporate mergers by 1889. Businesses soon scrambled to take advantage of the change.

BORN TO MAKE MONEY

While oil magnate John D. Rockefeller left his mark on America's oil business, other corporate tycoons did the same. One of the most powerful businessmen of his age was J. Pierpont Morgan, a financial wizard and steely player in the high stakes game of Wall Street finance. He became the most dominant and domineering financial banker in America during the Gilded Age. By 1912, Morgan held 12 directorships in 47 corporations. He once said, "America is good enough for me." When perennial presidential candidate, William Jennings Bryan, heard Morgan's words, he quipped, "Whenever he doesn't like it, he can give it back to us."[15]

J. Pierpont Morgan was born on April 17, 1837, in Hartford, Connecticut, the son of international banker, Junius Spencer

Morgan. The father represented old East Coast money. When Junius Morgan died, J.P. inherited $12 million. His mother, Juliet Pierpont, was the daughter of Unitarian minister John Pierpont. Young Morgan attended public schools in Hartford and later in Boston. He graduated from high school in 1854 and then traveled to Europe. By the late 1850s, Morgan joined the financial firm of Duncan, Sherman & Company in New York City. Four years later in 1861, he opened his own bank, J.P. Morgan & Company. By then, his father had been in business in London for several years and the younger Morgan became his father's business representative in New York. During the Civil War, he made a small fortune speculating in gold. He also received a contract from the War Department from which he bought defective rifles and then resold them to the government at a high profit.

Through the following decades, Morgan gained his reputation in the world of high finance. His father partnered him in 1864 with Charles Dabney in Dabney, Morgan & Company. Seven years later, he joined this company with a Philadelphia firm, Drexel & Company, as Drexel, Morgan & Company. Morgan remained a partner with Anthony Drexel until Drexel's death in 1893, after which the company became J.P. Morgan & Company. Throughout all these partnerships, Morgan was the driving force.

Morgan's early efforts as a businessman revolved around his underwriting new issues of railroad stocks and bonds. Railroad growth during the 1870s and 1880s was rapid, and wild speculation was a constant temptation. Morgan fought against such impulses and encouraged others to do the same. He soon gained a leading reputation as a cool-headed and clear-eyed investment analyst who guided the railroad industry through its expansive decades.

The Wall Street financier was able to sometimes bring dueling forces to the table and hammer out equitable agreements that were to everyone's advantage. For example, during the early 1880s, two great eastern railroads, the New York Central Railroad and the Pennsylvania Railroad (PR) began a rate war while trying to cut into each other's regional territories. Pennsylvania officials were planning to construct the West Shore line up the Hudson River next to the New York Central Railroad's main line, and NYCR officials were intending to do the same along the Pennsylvania's main artery. Concerned that these two railroads were hurting one another's business and profits, Morgan invited railroad officials from the NYCR and the Pennsylvania to meet with him onboard his private yacht, the *Corsaire III*, on the Hudson River. Morgan's yacht measured 300 feet from stem to stern and carried a crew of 70. Morgan loved sailing. Coming from old money, he once said about the newly rich men of his time: "You can do business with anyone but you can only sail a boat with a gentleman."[16]

The meeting was productive. Railroad officials agreed to stop their destructive rate wars. As to competing lines, the NYCR took over the West Shore line and the Pennsylvania got the South Penn, which it later abandoned. (Fifty years later, the Pennsylvania Turnpike included the Pennsylvania's route and tunnels in its new highway system.) Morgan was able to broker such agreements with these two powerful railroads because he was recognized as a financial powerhouse and because failing to cooperate with him might make if difficult for even the NYCR and the PR to find future financing.

Morgan also used his talents during the 1880s and 1890s to resuscitate failed or bankrupt railroads including the Reading, the Chesapeake & Ohio, the Southern, and the Erie. He was influential in placing on the boards of such railroads business friends who would run such lines efficiently and avoid rate wars and overbuilding. In time, J.P. Morgan was exerting a singular influence over 55,000 miles (88,709 kilometers) of railroads.

Like Rockefeller, Morgan was no fan of business and industrial competition. He despised competition in the railroad business, of course. When he and business ally James J.

Hill clashed in 1901 with regional railroad rival Edward H. Harriman over control of the Chicago, Burlington & Quincy Railroad (CB&Q) that serviced Chicago, St. Paul-Minneapolis, and Omaha, Wall Street nearly panicked. (Hill and Morgan controlled the Great Northern [GN] and the Northern Pacific [NP], while Harriman ran the Southern Pacific and the Union Pacific.) The titan businessmen sat down and hammered out agreements by which Harriman received a management share in the CB&Q. Morgan put the deal together by establishing a trust, the Northern Securities Corporation, which became the owner of the GN, the NP, and the CB&Q. To Morgan's way of thinking, such arrangements that limited competition and smoothed the way for efficient and profitable railroading were the primary goals.

As a Wall Street financial wizard, Morgan did not spend all his time cooking up railroad deals. By the 1890s, with industry on the dramatic rise, his financial firm, J.P. Morgan & Company, helped to finance important new industries. With the advent of the electrical age, Morgan financed the organization of General Electric (GE) in 1892, and a few years later, he was instrumental in raising investment capital in American Telephone & Telegraph (AT&T), as well as International Harvester, formerly the McCormick Harvester Works. His greatest business merger was the formation of Andrew Carnegie's steel company with other steel producers into a giant conglomerate, a trust that constituted the nation's first billion-dollar corporation—United States Steel.

Antitrust
Gains Popularity

With the success of J.P. Morgan's giant United States Steel, the stage was set for an extensive proliferation of similar business consolidations. Trusts had come to roost. Other industries, some encouraged by Morgan himself, altered themselves into trusts through mergers. Amalgamation in American business was the new driver. The impact of the merger craze would alter the system of American industry in a short period of time. The expansion of trusts in the United States also drew a backlash from the American people in the form of an antitrust movement.

A GRASSROOTS MOVEMENT

The movement that would, in time, pave the way for the antitrust sentiment in America had long-standing grassroots. Although the Sherman Antitrust Act would not become law until 1890, the seeds of the drive to rein in the monopolistic practices of trusts were planted during the 1870s and, of course, the 1880s. The movement against giant corporate power in America began on a small scale. Its first general target was the nation's railroads. As rail companies formed early pooling agreements during the 1860s and early 1870s, their immediate targets, the country's small business leaders and America's farmers, cried foul. They soon stood up and rallied in protest against the controlling corporations. In Illinois, the state's private farmers' association voted to pass a resolution in 1873 that expressed the angry concerns that so many in the country were experiencing: "Resolved, that the railways of the world, except in those countries where they have been held under the strict regulation and supervision of the government, have proved themselves arbitrary, extortionate, and as opposed to free institutions and free commerce between states as were the feudal barons of the middle ages."[1]

Many different and sometimes competing groups and organizations began to question the accumulation of wealth in the hands of a few. Labor organizations such as the Knights of Labor and the American Federation of Labor (AFL) preached in protest against the trusts, proclaiming that they held too much power over the economy of the United States. One of the leaders of the Knights, John Hayes, expressed his frustrations with America's ruling business class: "The great corporations, the trusts, with their capital, their machinery, special privileges and other advantages, are overwhelming the individual, reducing him to the condition of a mere tool, to be used in their great undertakings for their individual profit, and of no more consequence than a dumb piece of machinery."[2]

Wealth remained elusive for the vast majority of the country's working class. Only one percent of American families held seven out of every eight dollars that made up the American economy. Eighty percent of American families lived on the edge of poverty. By the same turn, a small number of individuals held much of the nation's wealth. For every one family with an

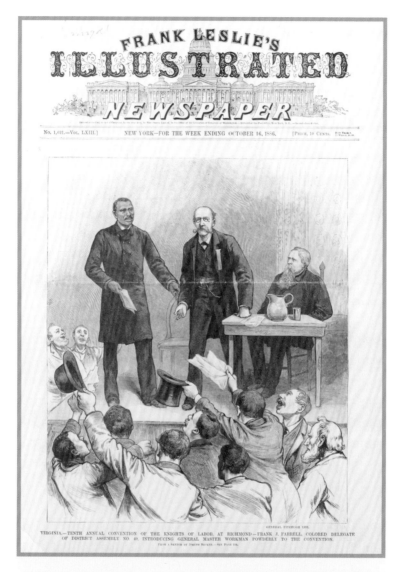

FRANK LESLIE'S ILLUSTRATED NEWSPAPER

No. 1,621.—Vol. LXIII.]   NEW YORK—FOR THE WEEK ENDING OCTOBER 16, 1886.   [Price, 10 Cents.

VIRGINIA.—TENTH ANNUAL CONVENTION OF THE KNIGHTS OF LABOR, AT RICHMOND—FRANK J. FARRELL, COLORED DELEGATE OF DISTRICT ASSEMBLY NO. 49, INTRODUCING GENERAL MASTER WORKMAN POWDERLY TO THE CONVENTION.

At the tenth annual convention in 1886 of the Knights of Labor in Richmond, Virginia, a delegate introduces General Master Workman Powderly to the convention. The group was formed to protest against the trusts, proclaiming that they held too much power over the economy of the United States.

income greater than $50,000 per year, 44 families in America managed to survive on less than $500 per year. That singular one percent of families often lived in absolute splendor and opulence. Andrew Carnegie may have been one of the wealthiest tycoons in America during the 1890s, but the vast majority of his mill and plant workers lived on less than $10 a week.

For so many of those living on so little, life was difficult. Working conditions at the country's mills, factories, and industrial plants were appalling, with little national or state legislation regulating abuses by owners. Housing conditions were miserable. One would-be reformer examined a poorer neighborhood in Chicago and described what he saw as "filthy and rotten tenements, the dingy courts and tumble down sheds, the foul stables and dilapidated outhouses, the broken sewer pipes, the piles of garbage fairly alive with diseased odors."[3]

Somewhere between America's opulent rich and its poorest people were the middle class who experienced neither of these two economic extremes. They had their issues, however. For many, despite a higher standard of living by the beginning of the twentieth century, the cost of that living was also going up, by 35 percent in less than 10 years of economic growth. While such middle class folks might enjoy some of life's simple pleasures, they did not see themselves as living the high life compared to the country's richest. An increasing percentage of middle class Americans were coming to believe that they had not yet achieved enough economic gain; that they had not received their fair share of the country's economic pie. For many, "the blame for their lack of economic advancement [fell] on the wealthy industrialists. They blamed the increasing number of trusts and monopolies in the United States."[4]

THE CALL FOR ECONOMIC REFORM

As the power of the trust movement and its negative impact on the economy became more obvious to Americans, they began to "mobilize politically, even if their efforts were, at first, small and almost inconsequential."[5] In 1884, the new Anti-Monopoly Party drew only 173,000 votes for president in that year's general election. Their candidate was Benjamin Butler, a former

Union general during the American Civil War. The party did not survive after the election, but several of the planks in its platform were taken up a few years later when the People's Party was established at a convention in Omaha, Nebraska, in 1892. It would remain for the Progressive Party of the early twentieth century to finally succeed in enacting much of the Anti-Monopoly Party's reforms.

Even though the Anti-Monopoly Party failed ultimately, the ball was at least rolling against the trusts by the mid-1880s. By 1888, the Republican Party, which, like the Democrats, had significant ties to big business and corruption in politics, included an antitrust element in its platform by officially positioning itself against "all combinations of capital organized in trusts."[6] That same year, the Democratic candidate, former president Grover Cleveland, also stood up against the trusts, claiming that the American people were being "trampled to death beneath [the] iron heel" of the monopolists.[7] Cleveland's Republican opponent, Benjamin Harrison, who won the 1888 election, referred to the trusts as "dangerous conspiracies against the public good."[8] By 1890, little had been done by the U.S. Congress to halt the actions of the trusts, but 21 state legislatures had enacted antitrust laws of one degree or another.

Even as a significant number of states created laws intended to curb the power of trusts, it was a patchwork effort at best. To bolster their legislative fronts, states also began to take trusts to court, suing them for "restraint of trade." In Nebraska, the state sued the whiskey trust; in Louisiana, the cottonseed trust; and in New York, the sugar trust. With Standard Oil based in Ohio, that state's attorney general sued the oil trust. Ultimately, the states won most of their cases. These victories did not succeed in putting even targeted trusts out of business. Instead, those who operated their corporations as trusts simply abandoned their corporate-trust structures and replaced them with other business organization devices such as mergers that might stand

(continues on page 72)

THE PENMEN OF ANTITRUSTISM

During the age of the great American monopolists and titans of the trust movement, several different groups decided to take significant and serious stands against amalgamation as a business tactic. One of the most influential groups included those who were not engaged directly in the business world at all. They were a unique category of protesters and social critics. They were not politicians, judges, or business leaders. They were men and women armed with the pen. They were writers.

An important group of writers, editors, and journalists contributed to this influential group who made the public aware of the abuses perpetuated on the American business scene. They drew the attention of an interested public toward such power-hungry corporate leaders. One of the most important among their number was Henry George, a talented newspaper writer from San Francisco. In 1879, George published his book, *Progress and Poverty*, which was destined to become one of the most important works on social criticism. At the heart of George's book, the author is concerned with an important question, one fundamental to the age: Why does growth in the American economy seem to parallel the expansion and certainly the perpetuation of poverty in this country? To George, the answer was simple.

Poverty in America was caused by a lopsided distribution of capital, especially land. Those with property were able to charge high rents to those who did not own land themselves, and they could do this without having markedly improved the property itself. George thought this was wrong, even immoral. Land in and of itself has no significant value. It is only when it is used (as in having someone live on it) that land becomes valuable. The existence of society, then, creates wealth. Rents collected by landlords, argued George, should be handed over to the government in the form of taxes and used for the public good. If land was taxed, wealth would be more evenly distributed and the monopolies would be driven out of business, even as the poor were lifted up economically.

In 1894, another book was critical of big business and the monopolists. Henry Demarest Lloyd, born in New York City, was a college-educated journalist, editor, and social critic. While in his thirties, Lloyd published articles exposing corruption in American business and politics, including "The Story of a Great Monopoly" in 1881 and "The Political Economy of Seventy-Three Million Dollars" the following year, both articles for the *Atlantic Monthly*. Such works would gain him the reputation in American history as the country's first investigative journalist.

His book, *Wealth Against Commonwealth*, was a scathing indictment of big business, especially Standard Oil Company. In his book, Lloyd itemizes the abuses perpetuated by the giant octopus company, making his work one of the first of the "muckraking" exposés that would become so popular in American journalism especially after the turn of the century. Lloyd's book was intended not only to inform the general public about the behind-the-scenes activities of big conglomerates in America but to motivate Americans to abandon their indifference and call for reform. The impassioned cries of Lloyd, George, and other social reformers and muckraking journalists did not fall on deaf ears. Public opinion did begin to turn against those who organized trusts and manipulated the American economy. The angry, national clamor led to the passage of the Interstate Commerce Act in 1887 and the Sherman Antitrust Act in 1890.

(continued from page 69)
up against the scrutiny of the judicial system. In other cases, a trust's board of directors might simply pack up and move out of a state and take up business in another state that did not yet have antitrust laws on its books.

State efforts to rein in their trusts only reinforced the necessity of national laws, legislation that would make it more difficult for trusts to "hide" by moving from state to state. Congress was largely motivated to such action because of the business practices of the nation's railroads. Across America, railroads had gained a reputation by the 1880s for their destructive practices and their tendency to gouge customers. Merchants and other business leaders complained of how the railroads commonly charged outlandish freight rates that would vary wildly from region to region, customer to customer. To make the point, a Sacramento newspaper published one railroad's freight rate schedule between Sacramento and several rail destinations in neighboring Nevada. The paper's report revealed that freight-wagon operators in business before the coming of the railroad had charged lower rates than the railroad did. There were other complaints. Railroads did not post their freight rates publicly; they charged more for hauling freight over short distances than over long distances; they charged small-time customers more per-ton-per-mile than large customers; and they offered kickbacks or under-the-table rebates to their favorite, big-time customers. To many Americans, all this made the railroads the transportation villains of the era.

State efforts to curb railroad abuses dated from the earliest days of the rail industry in America. The first state railroad commission was created in New Hampshire in 1844. Three additional states established state commissions by 1861. Following the Civil War, the concept of state control of railroads by commission became common, with 28 railroad agencies in place by 1896. These commissions typically took one of two forms. One type simply advised railroads when they were violating state laws. Usually, this type of agency had few teeth to enforce its decisions when railroads chose to ignore such state input. The second type of rail commission took the form of that found in Illinois by 1871. There, the state agency had more power to control railroad activities, including the authority to set railroad rates. Soon, additional Midwestern, agricultural states adopted laws establishing similarly empowered commissions.

THE COURTS STEP IN

The railroads, throughout the 1870s, often refused to abide by these state laws and challenged the state commissions at nearly every turn. This led to a series of court cases called the "Granger Cases," which often dealt with farmers who wanted railroads to be controlled and less abusive of them as a group. One of the most important of the Granger Cases was the Supreme Court decision *Munn v. Illinois* in 1877. Through this decision, the Court upheld a state's right to establish a commission empowered to regulate railroad rates, since railroad systems were "engaged in a public employment affecting the public interest."[9]

When Congress finally decided to move against such railroad abuses, they did so by passing an act that established the first federal regulatory agency in American history. The Interstate Commerce Act was passed in 1887, and its immediate target was the nation's railroads. Such legislation was necessary, since trains moved from one state to another. Thus, any state laws regulating railroads were difficult to enforce because rail traffic constituted interstate commerce. The act went straight to the point concerning its expectations. Railroad rates must be "reasonable and just," and rail companies must publish their rate schedules prominently in all train stations and depots. As to the unethical practice of handing out rebates and kickbacks to customers, the act declared it illegal.

Grange members meet in the woods near Winchester, Illinois, in 1873. The National Grange was founded by Oliver Kelley in 1867. By 1875, the movement had approximately 800,000 national members. Individual local Granges established cooperative grain elevators, mills, and stores. Together, they brought pressure on state legislatures to regulate the prices charged by railroads and grain elevators.

The act itemized the new restrictions and guidelines on railroad practices, but there were still legal issues yet to answer. How might the railroads interpret the phrase "reasonable and just" in establishing rail rates? A second issue revolved around the question of enforcement. Once the act became law, the public deluged the commission with complaints and requests for intervention and action by the Interstate Commerce Commission (ICC). Within months, the cases involving possible infractions by the railroads had mounted to over a thousand. It became clear that the ICC had no real enforcement means, except that of taking cases to federal courts. Even then, once a court decision was made, there was still no mechanism that could require the railroads to alter their practices.

As a result, the railroads typically ignored the ICC and its laws. They continued to charge excessive and varying rates even when the commission ordered them to stop. Congress could have prevented some of the agony and frustration experienced by the commissioners simply by having worded the law more precisely from the beginning. Perhaps there was truth in the claim that federal regulatory commissions were so new that the Congress did not really understand "exactly how to control interstate commerce."[10] The courts did not help. In many cases, the federal courts decided in favor of the railroads, giving the benefit of the doubt to the rail companies while judges questioned this new extension of federal power.

Things did not go well for the ICC in the beginning. Despite how conservative the measure actually was at the time, the Supreme Court of the 1890s was even more conservative. Between 1887 and 1905, the Supreme Court heard 16 ICC cases and decided in favor of the railroad parties in all but one. One railroad officer summed up the effect of the ICC on railroad practices, stating that "there is not a road in the country that can be accused of living up to the rules of the Interstate Commerce Law."[11]

This claim did not remain a matter of fact over the long haul. To claim that the ICC was an abject failure or a well-intended act that proved completely unenforceable is to say too much. The ICC was, in fact, "of epochal significance."[12] It would become the model for modern commissions that operated as extensions of the federal government, especially in the twentieth century. Those commissions would, in time, regulate much of the private sector including communications, power production, trade tariffs, and other important aspects of the modern American economy such as railroads. At the time of the ICC's creation, many Americans, including the congressmen who voted for the commission, could not imagine that this new act represented the beginning of a new course for the U.S. government, one that required federal authority to control whole portions of the economic system. The big picture ultimately tells the story of the value of the ICC. The commission did act, gathering railroad data as it investigated complaints against specific rail lines. It pushed and gained sway over the railroads by encouraging them to explain their rate differentials. In some cases, the railroads welcomed the new act because it gave them "an excuse in resisting the demands of shippers for special favors."[13] One of the great successes of the Interstate Commerce Act was to encourage railroad officials to recognize and live up to their responsibilities to the public they served.

The Sherman Antitrust Act

The Interstate Commerce Commission may not have accomplished enough in regulating the nation's railroads or managed to do so in a short enough period of time, but one thing was certain from the passage of the act: Public sentiment was being heard by the nation's congressmen. Regulation appeared to be the direction of the future, the new relationship between the U.S. government and at least portions of the nation's business sector. The swing was already in motion by the late 1880s; with the creation of the ICC and railroad regulation, a drive of equal importance and magnitude was afoot. The next rallying cry for government control was in favor of "antitrust."

THE CALL FOR ANTITRUST

One reason for this new call for limiting the power of the nation's business trusts was based on a new assumption concerning the nation's economy. Previously, many Americans who even thought about the nature of the market economy believed that as long as competition existed in the U.S. economy, the market would always be able to regulate itself on behalf of the interests of the public. Those same Americans, however, had now decided that the nation's trusts were destroying the element of competition. With this near elimination of competitiveness in the economy, as perceived by the American public, the trusts were doing damage to the public interest and nothing could stop them—at least, nothing short of government intervention. Such individuals looked at Standard Oil, saw it as a threat to competition and a self-regulating economy, and decided its rough shod, anticompetitive tactics needed to be corralled.

The call of the antitrust movement was first answered by the states, not the federal government. By 1890, 21 states had passed basic antitrust legislation in an attempt "to 'restore' competition either by incorporating antitrust clauses in their constitutions or by statute."[1] In some cases, the states merely worded artificial condemnations of the trusts without providing any context or teeth to bring about actual control of the monopolies. In other cases, state legislatures wrote out and voted in favor of strongly worded and detailed statutes that clearly identified the business practices that created and operated trusts, even as they set specific and stiff penalties for those who violated the new state laws. One of the most comprehensive was the 1889 antitrust act passed in Texas. The Lone Star State's legislation created a "dragnet of great sweep and close mesh"[2] that rendered illegal most combinations or trusts that had been created to limit trade, prevent competition, and control the level of production of a designated commodity while artificially setting its price.

Such laws typically did not have the immediate and intended results. Several of the states that passed such laws were Southern and Western (Texas could be considered both), where an inconsequential amount of industry existed. In addition,

This 1901 antitrust cartoon satirically depicts a little boy, representing the American public, while the big players, or corporate trusts, pelt him with baseballs.

such laws were rarely enforced or were difficult to effectively monitor. Also, most trusts were such large corporate structures that few did business in a single state. Instead, as with the example of Standard Oil, their corporate interests spread across state lines and even across regional lines. State laws stopped at state borders, even as conglomerate trusts did not.

(continues on page 83)

JOHN SHERMAN
(1823–1900)

The Man Behind the Proposal

John Sherman was born in Lancaster, Ohio, on May 10, 1823. By the age of 21, he had been admitted to the bar and was practicing law in Mansfield, Ohio. Although he grew up in the fiery age of national conflict concerning slavery and its expansion, he was not particularly interested in politics. That changed in 1854 with the passage of the Kansas-Nebraska Act, which opened up the northern portion of the old Louisiana Purchase territory to slavery, where it had been placed off limits more than 30 years earlier under the Missouri Compromise. Angered by this turn of events, he chose to enter politics.

The following year, Sherman was elected to Congress as a member of the newly formed Republican Party, whose platform included a plank in opposition to the Kansas-Nebraska Act. He served three terms in the House of Representatives until 1861 and then was elected to the Senate, where he served until 1877. The opening shots of the Civil War were fired just weeks after he was sworn in as a U.S. senator. (During the war, his brother, William Tecumseh Sherman, served as a Union general who became famous for his destructive campaign across Georgia and the Carolinas in 1864.)

In 1877, the veteran congressman and senator was tapped by President Rutherford B. Hayes to become the Republican president's secretary of the treasury. Following Hayes's single term as president, Sherman was again back in the Senate, having been reelected from Ohio the previous year. Sherman served in the Senate for the next 16 years. In 1897, he was again tapped by an incoming Republican president for a cabinet position, this time as William McKinley's secretary of state. The following year, Sherman stepped down from his post and retired into private life.

He died two years later after a long illness on October 22, 1900, in Washington, D.C.

For years, John Sherman wanted to be elected to the presidency. He threw his hat into the Republican ring in 1880 and again in 1888 at both Republican National Conventions. Both times, he failed to garner the nomination. Perhaps his involvement in several key political issues made him too controversial. He also seems to have lacked a warm personality, a trait always desired in a serious politician. (Back in Ohio, he had been nicknamed as "the Ohio Icicle.") After losing his 1888 bid for the Republican presidential nomination, he was consoled by former president Rutherford Hayes, who told him that "the man of great and valuable service . . . must be content to leave the Presidency to the less conspicuous and deserving."*

During Sherman's decades of government service, he was often associated with public finance and business issues. Through his career, he supported protective tariffs and fought against inflation in the national economy. He was typically not a strident politician who held extreme political views; instead he considered himself to be a moderate, one willing to compromise, with a give-and-take approach to making political deals. As a congressman and senator from Ohio, a state that was both rural and industrial, Sherman was "adept at balancing diverse interests."**

He gave his support to the 1862 Legal Tender Act, which authorized the issue of paper money during the Civil War, but he was also the designer of the Resumption Act in 1875, which called for a return to the gold standard in 1879 and the recall and conversion of paper money, known as greenbacks, back into gold. Not only did he push this legislation through the Senate,

(continues)

(continued)

after becoming Hayes's secretary of the treasury, he saw the conversion from greenbacks to gold become reality. Also concerning money issues, Sherman supported an unpopular congressional act that critics refer to as the "Crime of '73." This act removed silver coins from the treasury department's list of standard coins, a move designed to keep silver coins out of the country's currency because an overproduction of silver out West was causing the value of silver (and silver coins) to drop. In time, he came to believe that the U.S. money supply needed to have at least some silver coins, so he supported a bill that would bear his name as one of its sponsors—the Sherman
Silver Purchase Act of 1890. Under this act, the federal government began minting silver coins at the rate of 4.5 million ounces per month.

John Sherman believed in a vibrant, modern American economy and encouraged railroad expansion and industrial development through government subsidies and the protective tariff. He was also a supporter of limited government regulation of big businesses and large trusts. It became a cause for Sherman to call for the regulation, by the government, of interstate commerce. In 1890, he led the way in the passage of the Sherman Antitrust Act. The act prohibited business combinations that limited free trade, even if it was so vaguely worded that the legislation's impact was limited.

Ari Hoogenboom, ed. Encyclopedia of American History: The Development of the Industrial United States, 1870 to 1899. *Vol. VI. New York: Facts on File, 2003, p. 261.*
***Ibid.*

(continued from page 79)

As with the state laws that had earlier been passed to regulate interstate commerce but that had not succeeded, state laws intended to break up trusts also failed. The call soon went out, as it had three years earlier concerning the ICC, for federal action against amalgamations. The first federal antitrust bill made it to the floor of the House of Representatives in January 1888. The first such bill to reach the Senate appeared in May of the following year. The House proposal never saw the light of day. It was routed into committee and never emerged, along with 15 other similar proposals. The Senate bill did not fare much better.

A later bill did make some progress in the Senate. The senator who sponsored that proposed antitrust bill was a 34-year veteran of service to the U.S. government, who had first been sworn into office in December 1855, six years before the American Civil War and long before most of the trusts in the late 1880s had even come into existence. Republican Senator John Sherman from Ohio had also served as secretary of the treasury under President Hayes during the 1870s. He was a well-respected public servant who had long ago made his mark in the halls of governmental power, a man "uniformly reputed to be the ablest and most influential financial statesman in this country."[3]

That December, Senator Sherman did not waste any time presenting his bill on antitrustism. At the beginning of the first session of the 51st Congress, he introduced Senate Bill No. 1 on December 4, 1889. He had titled the bill that would bear his name, "A bill to declare unlawful, trusts and combinations in restraint of trade and production."[4] The bill was fairly direct in its descriptions of just what business systems it intended to limit. In the bill's Section 1, the scope of the bill was presented, targeting "all arrangements, contracts, agreements, trusts, or combinations between persons or corporations made with a view ... to prevent full and free competition ... are hereby declared to be against public policy, unlawful and void.[5]

THE SENATE CONSIDERS THE BILL

After the presentation of the bill to the Senate in December, the bill went for consideration to the Senate Finance Committee. By January 14, 1890, the bill emerged from that committee and was returned to the Senate. Five weeks later, on February 27, Sherman made a motion for the Senate to consider adopting the bill into law. The debate was on.

Once the motion for consideration passed, the first senator to take the floor was a Southerner, Senator James Zachariah George of Mississippi. The senator was a member of the Senate Judiciary Committee and a capable lawyer. (He had served as a Southern cavalry officer during the Civil War.) George described the proposed legislation as the most important piece of legislation under consideration by him and his colleagues, but of a nature that he could not support. George did not consider the bill's content to be constitutional. He also had serious doubts about the bill's efficiency. The senator's questions about the constitutionality of the antitrust bill rested on the scope of the bill, which he said intended to regulate not only interstate and foreign trade but some trade and manufacturing within the borders of several individual states as well.

In terms of the proposed law's efficiency, Senator George stated that, because it proposed to prohibit "arrangements, contracts, agreements, trusts, or combinations," the bill would only prohibit the plans to carry out such actions, not the actions themselves. George argued that once a business began taking such actions, such a corporation would only need to go to a foreign country to make its plans for creating a trust and then return to the United States and actually establish the trust in question, which would not violate the bill, since the Sherman bill did not "prohibit any overt acts which might be done in pursuance of such plans."[6] On this score, he assumed incorrectly, but his elaborately twisted logic and lawyerly arguments managed to convince many senators that the Sherman bill was inherently flawed and in need of being amended before becoming law.

This photograph of John Sherman was taken sometime between 1865 and 1880. Sherman was a statesman and legislator who served as the Republican representative from Ohio from 1855 to 1861; as senator from 1861 to 1877 and 1881 to 1897; as U.S. secretary of the treasury from 1877 to 1881; and as secretary of state from 1897 to 1898.

Three weeks later, on March 21, the Sherman bill was brought before the Senate again. At that point in time, Senator Sherman called for the presentation of a substitute bill to replace his original proposal. (The replacement had been written through Sherman's Committee on Finance.) In comparing the original bill with the substitute proposal, the differences were important. The Senate Finance Committee had attempted to strengthen the original bill by limiting its prohibitions to arrangements, contracts, agreements, trusts, or combinations established between citizens or corporations or a combination of the two, or different states, U.S. territories, or foreign countries. At the same time, another substitute for the Sherman bill was presented by a senator from Texas, Senator Reagan. Senators from various other states spoke, as well, lending their arguments to the debate over the Sherman bill and its alternatives. Senators from New York, Texas, Missouri, Iowa, and Colorado, along with Sherman from Ohio, each took the floor to argue their views that day. In every case, these congressional leaders lent their support to the proposed Sherman legislation.

Three days later, on March 24, the debate ensued again, with Senator David Turpie from Indiana speaking in favor of the Sherman bill. He stated:

> [T]he purpose of the bill of the Senator from Ohio is to nullify the agreements and obligations of the trusts; of these fraudulent combinations. I favor it. There is another purpose: to give to parties injured a civil remedy in damages for injury inflicted. I am in favor of that. Those are the two principal measures embraced in that bill. I am willing to go further, and I think Senators generally will also. There can be no objection to the proposition to nullify trust contracts. There can be no objection to giving a civil remedy for those injured thereby; and there ought to be still less objection to punishing penally those who are guilty of these fraudulent combinations.[7]

Not all senators favored the Sherman bill. Senator William Stewart of Nevada did take the floor to deliver an opposition speech. He was the only member of either house of Congress in opposition to the proposed Sherman antitrust legislation. His arguments were not comprehensive in any way, including his personal and professional statement: "I do not find any warrant in the Constitution for this particular class of legislation."[8] The Nevada senator went on to argue that the true course the Senate should take on the antitrust issue was through boycotts. He stated that the only effective means of meeting the challenge of the trusts would be for the people of the United States to form "counter combinations" among themselves, although he never explained just how such a thing might be accomplished. Although Senator Stewart presented his position seriously, almost no member of the Senate took him seriously. No one even referred to Stewart's remarks in opposition to Sherman's bill and no one even took the time to argue against it.

FINAL ARGUMENTS AND A VOTE

The final arguments of March 24 were delivered by Massachusetts senator George Hoar. He questioned whether the Sherman bill actually was designed to include all those responsible for creating and operating trusts in America. He was also critical of the bill's failure to include clear punishments for offenders. The bill offered an avenue to private citizens to file lawsuits against trusts for private damages, but that was about all. There was no apparent and effective way to steer violators of antitrust legislation to abide by the law. Even though Senator Hoar supported the bill in general, his overriding issue with the bill was that he did not want the Senate to pass "some crude, hasty legislation which does not cure the evil."[9]

After several more days of debate, it was proposed that the original Sherman bill and an amended form that included several changes, including the "Reagan Amendment," be sent to the Senate Judiciary Committee with instructions to report back to the Senate in 20 days. The Judiciary Committee did not take the nearly three weeks it was provided and returned its version of the proposed antitrust legislation to the Senate on April 2, 1890. (Ultimately the bill presented for Senate consideration in December 1889, even after four months of heated debate, had never come to a direct vote.) The revised version of the Sherman bill was, in almost every respect, in step with the original Sherman bill that had been presented to the Senate in December 1889. For that reason, perhaps, the revised version was still referred to as the "Sherman bill." Even though more debate did follow over the intervening weeks, few changes were made. By June 1890, the Congress had approved the Sherman Antitrust Act with only one dissenting vote between the House and Senate. The act was subsequently signed by President Benjamin Harrison on July 2.

A NEW ANTITRUST LAW

The sweep of the Sherman Act was clear. It declared illegal "every contract, combination in the form of trust or otherwise, or conspiracy, in restraint of trade or commerce among the several States, or with foreign nations."[10] Anyone who helped to facilitate or agreed to such business arrangements (the document stated "monopolize or attempt to monopolize"), if convicted, would be subject to fines of up to $1,000 and jail terms of up to one year. There was a damages portion to the new law, as well. If a private individual was "injured in his business or property" by such monopolies that were in violation of the act, that victim was entitled to triple damages in federal circuit court. The Sherman Antitrust Act had been written to straddle the business world by restraining combinations, making them both public and private offenses.[11]

One of the most significant aspects of the passage of the Sherman Antitrust Act was that it managed to get passed at all and remained relatively intact. The law intended to face down powerful commercial interests, including the nation's tycoons, such as Morgan and Rockefeller. Adding to the odds against passage was the fact that the 51st Congress was largely a conservative group of legislators. What, then, motivated these members of Congress to take such decisive action? It may have been that they were driven by the sheer magnitude of public opinion. Many Americans were angry at the nation's big trusts and had been so for years. It has been argued by some historians that in reality the new act did not intend to bring down the nation's trusts. These students of history have suggested that the Sherman Act was not that strong, that it was meant only as a token effort by Congress and that enforcing the act was never taken seriously. Still others have explained the bill's passage by suggesting that the subject of trusts was not considered to be that important, so the Congress passed a measure to address only a minor problem. In the end, it may be that all three theories concerning the passage of the Sherman Act are true. At any rate, despite the passage of this new antitrust legislation, "few persons expected the Sherman Act to produce drastic results."[12]

One additional explanation why the Sherman bill may have become law with relative unanimity within the ranks of Congress is because it did not make any significant changes in the structures of business law. Monopolies and trust-like constraints of business and competition were already fundamentally illegal. Such practices were considered, by American law, to be against public policy. Punishments for such amalgamations were already written into law. States that chartered corporations already had the recognized legal right and power to control those that constituted business concentrations. The primary impact and import of the Sherman Act was that it granted and recognized that same power on the part of the federal government. Now, the federal authorities were empowered to enforce the same principles of business that states had been granted long earlier. Again, the words of Senator George Hoar of Massachusetts ring true in reference to the Sherman Antitrust Act: "We have affirmed the old doctrine of the common law . . . and have clothed the United States courts with authority to enforce that doctrine . . . undertaking to curb by national authority an evil which under all our legislative precedents and policies, has been left to be dealt with either by the ordinary laws of trade or . . . by the States."[13]

Ultimately the decision by Congress to address the issue of trusts in America by passing a single piece of legislation while refusing to alter business law would have mixed results. It must be understood that this was a conscious decision made by both representatives and senators alike. Congress could have hemmed in the makers of the nation's trusts by adopting new patent laws or by reducing tariff rates or by requiring *federal* incorporation of larger businesses, those that operated across state or national lines, backed with strict controls over the business activities of such conglomerates. Congress chose not to do so.

The immediate result was that the Sherman Antitrust Act of 1890 "bore little immediate fruit."[14] Throughout the decade following the act's passage, the federal government only filed a small number of antitrust suits. In 1895, the U.S. Supreme Court put further limits on the scope of the Sherman Act in its decision titled *U.S. v. E.C. Knight Company*. In its decision, a majority on the Court decided that "monopolization of the manufacturing of an article by a single combine did not constitute restraint of interstate commerce per se, even if the goods later entered into such commerce."[15] (The severe depression that hit the country from 1893 until 1897 probably served to limit cases against monopolies, since the nation's economy had taken such a dramatic turn downward.) In the end, the Sherman Antitrust Act was proving inadequate to meet the very challenges for which the act was created. Monopolies typically remained in business into the twentieth century.

Antitrust in the New Century

With the passage of the Sherman Antitrust Act into law in 1890, the decade seemed poised to bring the era of combinations, amalgamations, monopolies, and trusts to an end. This was not the immediate result of the Sherman law. Congress had voted on a law that would become rarely enforced and even blocked by the conservative justices of the U.S. Supreme Court.

A PROLIFERATION OF TRUSTS

By 1904, 75 percent of the trusts in the United States had been established since 1898, eight years following the passage of the act that some had hoped would rein in the power of the country's trusts. The march of America's monopolies had continued, sometimes at an even quicker pace than before the passage of the Sherman Antitrust Act. With the end of the depression of 1893 in 1897, the following year saw a great proliferation in the number of trusts. As a result of that amalgamation trend, the structure of American industry changed in a short period of time. At the end of the Civil War in 1865, monopolies or trusts were almost nonexistent in the country. Competition was the norm, and no single company or business dominated any given field of production.

By 1904, however, corporate trusts were more in style. That year, one or two giant firms, put together in large part by merger, controlled at least half the output in 78 different industries. In the extreme growth industry of American railroading, the last third of the nineteenth century had almost managed to end competition. Just prior to the outbreak of the Civil War in 1860, approximately 20 railroads competed in the railroad market place. By 1900, as a result of mergers, the railroad industry was led by two great rail corporations. By the turn of the century, J. D. Rockefeller had cornered 80 percent of the oil market. Mergers affected every aspect of the American economy, even those parts that might seem inconsequential. In the biscuit and cracker industry, several competing companies were all rolled into one big corporate firm to create a single, dominant force in the nation's cracker producers—the National Biscuit Company.

American business was also changing in other key ways through the latter years of the nineteenth century. Not only were businesses amalgamating into single, noncompetitive entities, the sheer size of American corporations was gigantic. During the Civil War, the country probably could not boast a single company with a worth of $10 million or greater. Even as late as 1896, the year of William McKinley's election and the last full year of the depression, there were probably still not as many as a dozen companies valuated at $10 million. The early years of the twentieth century changed all that. By 1904, as the trust trend was peaking, the number of companies worth

$10 million or greater reached 300. Together, they controlled $20 billion in assets, a sum equal to 40 percent of the country's industrial wealth. Morgan and Rockefeller each controlled a banking group that included 34 directors of a dozen American corporations that held more than $22 billion in assets.

LITTLE SUPPORT FOR THE SHERMAN LAW

What of the era's presidents? Did they provide support for the Sherman Antitrust Act or were they equally conservative and such friends of big business that they acted as accessories to the trusts rather than enforcers of the law? The answer is both. Certainly presidents Benjamin Harrison (1889–1893) and Grover Cleveland (1893–1897) did little in support of the Sherman law. Harrison had spoken out in favor of the antitrust legislation, but he did not actively pursue cases against trusts. In fact, Harrison and many Republicans supported a high protective tariff for domestic producers. The campaign that ended with Harrison's election (he ran against Cleveland that year) did not signal the rise of a president who would really lend a serious hand to antitrust legislation even if he did agree to sign the Sherman Antitrust Act in 1890. Although Cleveland was not reelected in 1888, he ran a third time in 1892 and became the nation's first nonconsecutively elected chief executive. In fact, he defeated Harrison in 1892 by a decisive margin of 400,000 votes.

With the Sherman Act almost two-and-a-half years old by the time Cleveland took office, he did not use the act much. He was forced to deal with other matters of greater importance to the general economy. Between 1893 and 1897, the country's economy experienced a significant downturn, amounting to a major depression. The times were not right for the federal government to step on big business's toes or to interrupt the economy in any way. The decade would offer little true antitrust efforts on the part of the federal government throughout the remainder of the 1890s. (Republicans managed to elect

President William McKinley delivers a speech on tariffs and trade in Buffalo, New York, a day before he was shot at the Pan-American Exposition in Buffalo on September 6, 1901. McKinley died eight days later.

their candidate, William McKinley, in 1896, a conservative supporter of even higher tariffs.)

Even as McKinley was reelected in 1900, the path followed by the nation's trusts was still widely walked. Things were about to change. Just months into his second term, on September 6, a lone gunman (a short, slender, 28-year-old anarchist named Leon Czolgosz) caught up with McKinley at a world's fair in Buffalo. He shot the president in the Pan-American Exposition's Temple of Music where McKinley was receiving visitors in a long receiving line. (Czolgosz hid his short-barreled .32 revolver under a handkerchief that covered his right hand.) Although known for being a conservative Republican, McKinley had just delivered a speech in which he indicated that he was about to steer his party away from the long-standing tradition of supporting high tariffs.

McKinley lived a week after the shooting and died in the early morning hours of September 14. For the next 12 hours, the United States officially had no president, for Vice President Theodore Roosevelt was off camping in the Adirondack Mountains of upstate New York, and had to be tracked down by a local guide. Roosevelt rode all night in a horse-drawn buckboard to a waiting train that delivered him to Buffalo where he was sworn in later that day. With the rise of New Yorker Theodore Roosevelt to the White House, the unguarded days of the nation's trusts were about to be challenged.

A PRESIDENT OF THE PEOPLE

Roosevelt soon became the man of the moment. Most American presidents before him had rarely stepped out into the direct path of the country's powerful business leaders; however, Roosevelt was born for such confrontations. Not only was he a firm believer in the American people and the ideals of republican government, but he was also a great supporter of using the power of the federal government for the good of the majority of its citizens. Although he came from a wealthy New

York family whose Dutch roots extended back to seventeenth-century New Amsterdam, he often spoke out against the nation's business and corporate leaders whom he perceived were not acting in the people's interests. In speeches, he would refer to the "wealthy criminal class," the "malefactors of great wealth," the "conscienceless swindlers," and "the "infernal thieving trusts." (At the same time, he had no room for anticapitalist radicals, the nation's anarchists and socialists he would call "cowards," "shrill eunuchs," and "pin-heads and cranks of ugly radicalism."[1]

He was not a president interested in bringing down those self-serving businessmen and women who led American economic interests. (Although most of the nation's richest business leaders at the turn of the century were men, Hetty Green was a real estate and stock tycoon who was worth nearly $200 million when she died in 1913.) Roosevelt was not interested in tearing the house down, just making it livable for more than one group. His goal as president was to rein in American business power, to regulate it, not destroy it. The American people were being victimized by the trusts and had been for decades. He sought redress for the people. To do so, he first had to fight those within his own political party, those conservative members who had maintained a hands-off policy to the big money interests. Roosevelt, almost overnight, became the great symbolic leader of a reform movement that unfolded during the first 20 years of the twentieth century. It would be known as Progressivism, and it would mark an era of reform on all levels in America, from controlling the country's powerful trusts to cleaning up corrupt government to passing social legislation allowing women to vote.

As he set out to take the trusts on, Roosevelt found himself going against some of the wealthiest interests in the country; individuals who had amassed their fortunes years earlier and become spectacularly wealthy in the meantime. Old John Rockefeller, in 1901, was worth approximately $200 million, and his oil business was virtually unchallenged in America. Andrew Carnegie sold his interests in his steel company that year for nearly half a billion dollars to J. Pierpont Morgan, who was among the wealthiest men on the earth. Even though such individuals were men of great wealth (America was home to 4,000 millionaires in 1901), there were 5.5 million families with annual incomes of less than $150 (an amount equivalent to approximately $5,000 today). Those millionaires represented less than 0.0001 of 1 percent of America's population, but they controlled 20 percent of the nation's wealth. One percent of American families owned half of the country's wealth. This imbalance of wealth and poverty was one of Roosevelt's motivations.

At the time that Roosevelt took office in 1901, approximately 20 business leaders dominated the American financial and industrial landscape. They lived by the accumulated power of their corporate trusts. Their reach of power was absolutely extensive:

> They flaunted a power at least as great as the president's. They decided where Americans would work and what they would pay for steel, oil, petroleum, rail freight, farm machinery, glass, rubber and tin cans; for tobacco, sugar, coal, beef, dressed meat, starch, school slates, flour, whisky, insurance, chewing gum and coffins. Hundreds of small businessmen claimed in the courts that they had been unfairly ruined by larger competitors operating through combinations, the kaleidoscopic masks . . . of monopoly power.[2]

Despite the existence of the Sherman Antitrust Act of 1890, trusts continued to operate with impunity. These monopolies or combinations were still huge interstate corporations, and later were holding companies, were run by boards of directors who were left by the federal government to carry out business as usual. State laws limiting the power of the trusts were in

Theodore Roosevelt (1858–1919) is shown here in 1904. Vice President Roosevelt became president after McKinley died. Roosevelt was nicknamed the "trustbuster" when his administration began to target the most powerful trusts in the U.S. economy.

place, but they were unable to halt the massive economic power of control held by the trusts. Such money titans as J. Pierpont Morgan, owner of United States Steel and one of the country's richest men, felt no qualms about the trusts. In his view, "I owe the public nothing."[3] Morgan saw great good in negotiating rivals in a given industry into a "community of interest," which was simply code for "trust," which would allow competitors "to cut the public's throat rather than one another's."[4]

MOVES MADE ON MORGAN

It was this sort of nonchalant regard of the American public that infuriated President Roosevelt. As a man of relative wealth, and leader of the United States, he thought it his duty to serve as an agent of the people. He made his first moves against the monopolistic interests within his first five months in office. His charge began with a speech he delivered following a Washington press dinner in the spring of 1902, in which he spoke critically of J. Pierpont Morgan. Then, on March 10, he gave instructions to his attorney general, Philander C. Knox, to file an antitrust suit against one of Morgan's most recently formed railroad conglomerations, the Northern Securities Company, a holding company formed by combining three competing railroads (the Great Northern, the Northern Pacific, and the Chicago, Burlington, & Quincy) into one large monopoly with little competition between the Great Lakes and the Pacific Coast.

When J. Pierpont Morgan was informed of the suit, he was outraged. He made an immediate trip to the White House to talk directly with President Roosevelt, saying that if there was a problem to be worked out, "send your man [Knox] to my man [naming one of his lawyers] and we can fix it up." To Morgan, such issues did not require law suits. The needs of business and politics could be accomplished as with any other deal. Roosevelt and Knox would have none of it, however. An angry Roosevelt responded to Morgan with a strong admonition: "That can't be done." Knox made things even more clear to the Wall Street mogul: "We don't want to fix it up, we want to stop it."[5]

At first, Morgan and almost all other business tycoons in America were angered and frustrated. The announcement of Roosevelt's intentions hit the security markets hard. One newspaper, the *Detroit Free Press*, wrote a taunting line, aimed at the nation's business leaders: "Wall Street is paralyzed at the thought that a President of the United States should sink so low as to enforce the law."[6] When business leaders realized that Roosevelt intended to break up the Northern Securities Company by invoking the tenets of the Sherman Antitrust Act, they took a degree of comfort. The law had laid nearly dormant for more than a decade. Many Americans believed the law did not even exist any longer or, at least, that it might as well be dead. The courts, including the Supreme Court, had typically turned a deaf ear to cases based on the law. Concerning industrial trusts, the Supreme Court had decided in 1895 that the Sherman Act only forbade the restraint of interstate trade or commerce. The court defined "manufacturing" as neither.

TEDDY ROOSEVELT, THE TRUSTBUSTER

Roosevelt's efforts did pay off. Despite the expectations of many people, Attorney General Knox had won his case. In 1904, the Supreme Court, by a vote of 5 to 4, reversed its earlier decision and decided on the part of the federal government. The Northern Securities Company was, indeed, a trust, and it would have to broken up. Roosevelt lifted the decision up as a victory for the American people, considering "it was as important a ruling in the interests of the people against monopoly as the Dred Scott case had been in the interests of the people against slavery."[7] The nation generally agreed. That November, Roosevelt was reelected president by a significant majority. "Teddy" had become America's trustbuster.

Throughout his presidency, Roosevelt continued his march against the trusts, ordering his Justice Department to file more antitrust cases then the three presidents before him (Harrison, Cleveland, and McKinley) combined. In all, the Roosevelt administration filed 44 antitrust suits against big business combinations. During his presidency, the Justice Department filed suit against such monopolistic giants as DuPont Corporation, the Chicago meat packers, the American Tobacco Company, and even Standard Oil Company. The latter suit was not adjudicated until 1911, when Roosevelt was no longer in office. Although the court decided to dissolve the Standard Oil Trust, one wing of the trust, the Standard Oil Company of New Jersey, quickly reorganized itself into a holding company, allowing it to retain control over some 70 companies that had technically been severed from the parent company following the court's decision.

On one level, Roosevelt's intention was to bring the trusts under the control of the federal government, then set the business world back on a course of true free enterprise and laissez-faire economics. Despite his intentions, Roosevelt never intended to attack and bring down all the nation's trusts. "This is an age of combination," Roosevelt would write on one occasion, "and any effort to prevent all combination will be not only useless, but in the end vicious."[8] Theodore Roosevelt reserved his assaults on the trusts for those trusts that he believed were abusing their economic power. Those trusts that he thought acted responsibly toward the American people, offering the populace some ultimate advantage by their mere existence, he left alone. In some situations, he chose not to send his Justice Department after a certain trust, but elected to try to negotiate and redefine the trust's parameters and impact on the American people. To encourage and allow that sort of bargaining, in 1904 Roosevelt established a Bureau of Corporations under the jurisdiction of the Department of Commerce and Labor, which he had only established the previous year.

Roosevelt not only worked to make the Sherman Antitrust Act a viable, meaningful, and powerful tool of the federal government but also sought to expand the regulatory reach of the Interstate Commerce Commission. In 1903, at Roosevelt's bidding, Congress passed the Elkins Act, which eliminated rebates issued by railroad companies. Three years later, he saw to the passage of the Hepburn Act, which was named for Senator William P. Hepburn of Iowa. The act empowered the ICC to set railroad rates and review railroad accounts and financial records. The Hepburn Act made it clear that a strong president, with the backing of the American public, could bring the railroads down a notch or two.

When Theodore Roosevelt left the White House in 1909, the days of trustbusting were not over. His successor, former secretary of war William Howard Taft, also pursued the destruction of the trusts. His support of the Sherman Antitrust Act led him to state: "We are going to enforce that

ANTITRUSTISM THROUGH THE TWENTIETH CENTURY

With the passage of the Sherman Antitrust Act in 1890, the country moved into a prolonged era in which the giant monopolies would at first scoff at and then take seriously the federal government's efforts to limit the power that these trusts possessed. With the Progressivism of Theodore Roosevelt, Taft, and Wilson, the great amalgamations began to find it more difficult to operate without the government threatening to break up such business combinations. In 1914, the Clayton Antitrust Act and the Federal Trade Commission provided greater legal grounds for the government to file antitrust suits.

By 1920, the U.S. Supreme Court began to apply a new maxim to deciding antitrust suits, however. It was called the "rule of reason," and it represented a new interpretation of the Sherman Act. This new rule was based on the logic that only "unreasonable" restraints of trade, through acquisitions, mergers, exclusionary tactics, and aggressive pricing, should be defined as violations of the Sherman Antitrust Act. This new guideline altered the scope of the Sherman law, making it easier for large companies and corporations to operate.

law or die in the attempt."⁹ In some ways, Taft was an even greater advocate for tearing down the nation's monopolies than Roosevelt. Unlike Roosevelt, Taft did not hold back and allow "pet trusts" to continue. In fact, although Taft served only one term as president to Roosevelt's two terms, Taft managed to order the filing of twice as many antitrust suits as Roosevelt. The Taft administration even attacked United States Steel. This move proved embarrassing to the former president. In 1907, at the height of a national depression, President Roosevelt had given the green light to United States Steel to acquire the Tennessee Coal and Iron Company, a move Roosevelt considered

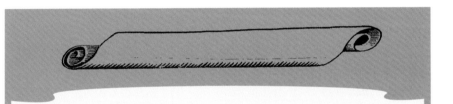

That position of the Court's did not stand long, however. In 1945, the Court reversed itself through a case involving the Aluminum Company of America. In its decision, the Court declared that the size and structure of a corporate trust provided sufficient grounds for antitrust action. Since that decision, cases against monopolies have been infrequent. In 1976, a new federal law, the Hart-Scoss-Rodino Antitrust Improvement Act, allowed regulators to investigate mergers for antitrust violations, but few mergers were blocked.

During the 1980s, the Justice Department filed suit against the American Telephone & Telegraph Company (AT&T), resulting in the breakup of the giant telephone company into seven regional "Baby Bells." In the 1990s, Microsoft Corporation was targeted by the U.S. Justice Department for antitrust violations. Although the courts decided against Microsoft in 2000, claiming the company had attempted to establish a monopoly in Internet-browser software, the court decision was overturned in 2001 in an appeals court.

important at the time, due to the downturn in the national economy. Taft's suit against United States Steel was partially based on that 1907 Roosevelt-approved merger.

NEW ANTITRUST MOVES

In 1912, Taft lost reelection to the Democratic candidate, Woodrow Wilson, former governor of New Jersey and Progressive reformer. Wilson was an even greater advocate for attacking the nation's trusts than Taft or Roosevelt. Even though Roosevelt had supported the policy of regulating the trusts specifically and big business generally, Wilson was not a supporter of government regulation of corporate America. He chose to pursue his economic strategy through the Sherman Antitrust Act and other laws intended to break up monopolies. This approach, Wilson argued, resulted in the restoration of competition, provided for more efficient business operations, and encouraged "individualism that had made America a rich and powerful nation."[10] In Wilson's words: "If monopoly persists, monopoly will always sit at the helm of government. I do not expect monopoly to restrain itself. If there are men in this country big enough to own the government of the United States, they are going to own it."[11] The Wilson years witnessed two important laws intended to provide support to the Sherman Antitrust Act, both passed in 1914. The Federal Trade Commission was established with the power to conduct investigations of giant business corporations. The Clayton Antitrust Act, the most important piece of legislation limiting trusts since the Sherman Act, made "interlocking directorates" illegal. These were corporate structures that had allowed the directors of one corporation to be directors of other corporations in the same product area. Clayton also provided that the directors of a company that violated the antitrust laws could be held personally accountable for their actions. Peripherally, but importantly, the Clayton Act also stated that labor unions should not be defined as "combinations in restraint of trade."

Antitrustism would continue in America throughout the twentieth century and beyond. New laws would be passed, and other presidents would take hard lines against the combinations of business power and greed. Stands taken throughout the century and beyond since the passage of the Sherman Antitrust Act rest on the shoulders of that original, groundbreaking piece of legislation. It had come to life surrounded by a thousand trusts, each hungrily holding onto its corner of the American economic scene. The Sherman Act, however, with time on its side, had worked to bring down the self-interested tycoons and to tame those robber barons who had at one time seemed so invincible.

CHRONOLOGY

1607 Jamestown is established as first permanent English settlement in North America, and as a joint-stock investment venture, beginning the British colonial period.

1700 New England has a fleet of 2,000 shipping and fishing vessels serving as an important part of the colonial region's economy.

1790 British immigrant and mechanic Samuel Slater builds one of America's first water-powered textile mills.

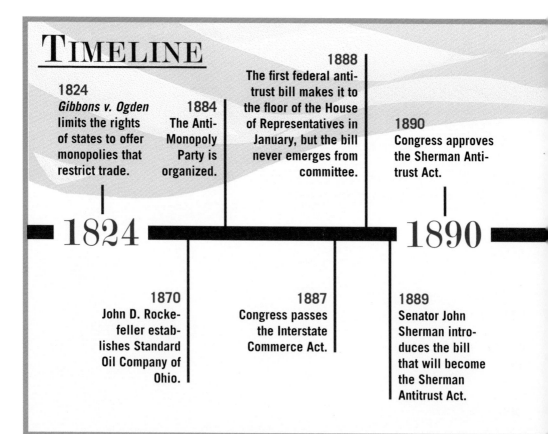

TIMELINE

1824
Gibbons v. Ogden limits the rights of states to offer monopolies that restrict trade.

1884
The Anti-Monopoly Party is organized.

1888
The first federal anti-trust bill makes it to the floor of the House of Representatives in January, but the bill never emerges from committee.

1890
Congress approves the Sherman Anti-trust Act.

1824 — 1890

1870
John D. Rockefeller establishes Standard Oil Company of Ohio.

1887
Congress passes the Interstate Commerce Act.

1889
Senator John Sherman introduces the bill that will become the Sherman Antitrust Act.

1790s   Close to a dozen factories and mechanized mills are built in the United States.

1791   America's first secretary of the treasury, Alexander Hamilton, presents a report to Congress encouraging congressional support for manufacturing; the First Bank of the United States receives its first charter.

1793   Northerner Eli Whitney invents the cotton gin, paving the way for the nation's cotton culture of the nineteenth century.

1819   The U.S. Supreme Court decides a case encouraging uniform bankruptcy laws.

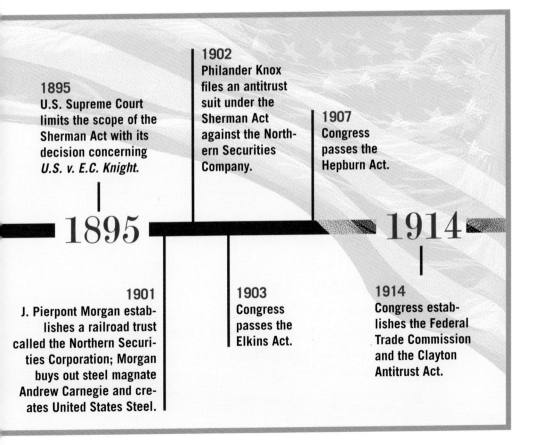

1895
U.S. Supreme Court limits the scope of the Sherman Act with its decision concerning *U.S. v. E.C. Knight.*

1902
Philander Knox files an antitrust suit under the Sherman Act against the Northern Securities Company.

1907
Congress passes the Hepburn Act.

1895

1914

1901
J. Pierpont Morgan establishes a railroad trust called the Northern Securities Corporation; Morgan buys out steel magnate Andrew Carnegie and creates United States Steel.

1903
Congress passes the Elkins Act.

1914
Congress establishes the Federal Trade Commission and the Clayton Antitrust Act.

1824   *Gibbons v. Ogden* limits the rights of states to offer monopolies that restrict trade.

1830   The first American railroad is built; before the end of the decade, the country will witness more 3,300 miles (5,323 kilometers) of railroad track laid; the United States is on the path to becoming an industrialized country.

1860s   Jay Gould begins investing in railroads.

1870   America is home to approximately 500,000 business firms; John D. Rockefeller establishes Standard Oil Company of Ohio.

1877   Supreme Court decides the Granger Cases, including *Munn v. Illinois,* which upheld a state's right to establish a commission to regulate railroad rates.

1879   Henry George publishes *Progress and Poverty.*

1880s   United States witnesses proliferation of corporations and industrialization; during that decade, pooling arrangements become commonplace.

1882   Rockefeller's chief attorney, Samuel C.T. Dodd, organizes the Standard Oil Company as a trust.

1884   The Anti-Monopoly Party is organized and draws 173,000 votes during the presidential election.

1887   Congress passes the Interstate Commerce Act.

1887–1905   U.S. Supreme Court hears 16 ICC cases and decides 15 of them on behalf of railroad plaintiffs.

1888   Both the Republican and Democratic parties include antitrust planks in their platforms; the first federal antitrust bill makes it to the floor of the House of Representatives in January, but the bill never emerges from committee.

1889   Senator John Sherman introduces Senate Bill No. 1 in December, which will become the Sherman Antitrust Act.

1890   Railroad track mileage in America reaches 185,000; 21 states have enacted antitrust laws; Congress approves the Sherman Antitrust Act.

1894   Henry Demarest Lloyd publishes *Wealth Against Commonwealth.*

1895   U.S. Supreme Court limits the scope of the Sherman Act with its decision concerning *U.S. v. E.C. Knight.*

1901   J. Pierpont Morgan establishes a railroad trust called the Northern Securities Corporation; Morgan buys out steel magnate Andrew Carnegie and creates United States Steel.

1902   President Theodore Roosevelt's attorney general, Philander Knox, files an antitrust suit under the Sherman Act against the Northern Securities Company.

1903   Congress passes the Elkins Act, which eliminates rebates issued by railroad companies.

1904   Seventy percent of all industrial plants in America operate as corporations; Bureau of Corporations is put under the jurisdiction of the Department of Commerce and Labor.

1907   Congress passes the Hepburn Act, which empowers the ICC to set railroad rates and review railroad accounts and financial records.

1912   J. Pierpont Morgan holds 12 directorships in 47 corporations.

1914   Congress establishes the Federal Trade Commission and the Clayton Antitrust Act.

1920 U.S. Supreme Court applies maxim called the "rule of reason" for deciding antitrust suits.

1945 U.S. Supreme Court reverses the "rule of reason" through a case involving the Aluminum Company of America.

1976 Newly passed Hart-Scoss-Rodino Antitrust Improvement Act allows regulators to investigate mergers for antitrust violations.

1980s Justice Department forces the American Telephone & Telegraph Company to break up.

2000 Court decision determines Microsoft is in violation of antitrust laws; the following year, the court's decision is overturned.

NOTES

CHAPTER 1

1. James Kirby Martin, *America and Its People.* New York: Harper-Collins College Publishers, 1993, p. 552.
2. Ibid.
3. Ibid.
4. Harold Evans, *The American Century.* New York: Alfred Knopf, 1998, p. 78.
5. Martin, *America and Its People,* p. 552.
6. Evans, *The American Century,* p. 78.
7. Ibid.
8. Martin, *America and Its People,* p. 552.
9. Evans, *The American Century,* p. 78.

CHAPTER 2

1. Robert Heilbroner and Aaron Singer, *The Economic Transformation of America, 1600 to the Present.* Fort Worth: Harcourt Brace College Publishers, 1994, p. 46.
2. Ibid., p. 67.
3. Ibid.
4. Martin, *America and Its People,* p. 278.
5. Ibid., p. 277.

CHAPTER 3

1. Martin, *America and Its People,* p. 278.
2. Ibid., p. 277.
3. Ibid., p. 276.

CHAPTER 4

1. Martin, *America and Its People,* p. 554.
2. Ibid., p. 555.
3. Heilbroner and Singer, *The Economic Transformation of America,* p. 155.
4. Ibid.
5. Martin, *America and Its People,* p. 556.

CHAPTER 5

1. Heilbroner and Singer, *The Economic Transformation of America,* p. 157.
2. Ibid.
3. Ibid.
4. John Tipple, "The Robber Baron in the Gilded Age," in *The Gilded Age,* ed. H. Wayne Morgan. New York: Syracuse University Press, 1970, p. 36.
5. Martin, *America and Its People,* p. 563.
6. Ibid., p. 564.
7. Ibid., p. 565.
8. Heilbroner and Singer, *The Economic Transformation of America,* p. 201.
9. Martin, *America and Its People,* p. 565.
10. Ibid., p. 566.
11. Ibid.
12. Heilbroner and Singer, *The Economic Transformation of America,* p. 203.
13. Ibid., p. 205.
14. Ibid.

15. Evans, *The American Century*, p. 79.
16. Ibid.

CHAPTER 6

1. Heilbroner and Singer, *The Economic Transformation of America*, p. 221.
2. Ibid., p. 211.
3. Martin, *America and Its People*, p. 724.
4. Heilbroner and Singer, *The Economic Transformation of America*, p. 208.
5. Ibid., p. 221.
6. John A. Garraty, *The New Commonwealth, 1877–1890*. New York: Harper Torchbooks, 1968, p. 123.
7. Ibid.
8. Ibid.
9. Edward L. Ayers, et al. *American Passages: A History of the United States*. Belmont, Calif.: Thomson Higher Education, 2007, p. 502.
10. Garraty, *The New Commonwealth, 1877–1890*, p. 121.
11. Ibid., pp. 119–120.
12. Ibid., p. 120.
13. Ibid.

CHAPTER 7

1. Ibid., p. 122.
2. Ibid.
3. Albert H. Walker, *History of the Sherman Law of the United States of America*. New York: Equity Press, 1910, p. 1.
4. *Congressional Record*, 51st Cong., 1st sess., p. 96.
5. Ibid., p. 1765.
6. Walker, *History of the Sherman Law*, p. 8.
7. *Congressional Record*, p. 2558.
8. Ibid., p. 2565.
9. Garraty, *The New Commonwealth, 1877–1890*, p. 124.
10. Ibid.
11. Ibid.
12. Ibid., p. 125.
13. Ibid.
14. Ibid., p. 126.
15. Ibid., p. 127.

CHAPTER 8

1. Evans, *The American Century*, p. 71.
2. Ibid., p. 80.
3. Ibid.
4. Ibid.
5. Ibid.
6. Ibid.
7. Ibid.
8. Martin, *America and Its People*, p. 741.
9. Ibid., p. 743.
10. Heilbroner and Singer, *The Economic Transformation of America*, p. 219.
11. Richard Hofstadter, *The Age of Reform*. New York: Vintage Press, 1955, p. 232.

BIBLIOGRAPHY

Allen, Frederick Lewis. *The Big Change: America Transforms Itself, 1900–1950*. New York: Harper & Brothers, 1952.

Ayers, Edward L., et al. *American Passages: A History of the United States*. Belmont, Calif.: Thomson Higher Education, 2007.

Beatty, Jack. *Age of Betrayal: The Triumph of Money in America, 1865–1900*. New York: Alfred A. Knopf, 2007.

Commager, Henry Steele, ed. *The American Destiny: An Illustrated History of the United States*. Vol. 10, *The Rise of an Industrial Giant*. London: Orbis, 1986.

———. *The American Destiny: An Illustrated History of the United States*. Vol. 11, *Progress and Poverty*. London: Orbis, 1986.

Editors of Time-Life. *Prelude to the Century: 1870–1900*. Alexandria, Va.: Time-Life Books, 1999.

Evans, Harold. *The American Century*. New York: Alfred Knopf, 1998.

Garraty, John A. *The New Commonwealth, 1877–1890*. New York: Harper Torchbooks, 1968.

Goldfield, David. *The American Journey: A History of the United States*. Upper Saddle River, N.J.: Pearson/Prentice Hall, 2004.

Gould, Lewis L. *Reform and Regulation: American Politics from Roosevelt to Wilson*. New York: Alfred A. Knopf, 1986.

Heilbroner, Robert, and Aaron Singer. *The Economic Transformation of America, 1600 to the Present*. Fort Worth: Harcourt Brace College Publishers, 1994.

High, Jack C., and Wayne E. Gable. *A Century of the Sherman Act: American Opinion, 1890–1990.* Fairfax, Va.: George Mason University Press, 1992.

Hoogenboom, Ari, ed. *Encyclopedia of American History: The Development of the Industrial United States, 1870 to 1899.* Vol. VI. New York: Facts on File, 2003.

Letwin, William. *Law and Economic Policy in America: The Evolution of the Sherman Antitrust Act.* New York: Random House, 1965.

Martin, James Kirby. *America and Its People.* New York: HarperCollins College Publishers, 1993.

May, Ernest R. *The Progressive Era.* Vol. 9, *1901–1917.* New York: Time Incorporated, 1964.

Roark, James L. *The American Promise: A History of the United States.* Vol. I, *A New World to Conquer.* Boston: Bedford/St. Martin's, 2002.

Simmons, Andre. *The Sherman Antitrust Act and Foreign Trade.* University of Florida Monographs, no. 16, Fall 1962. Gainesville: University of Florida Press, 1963.

Smith, Page. *A People's History of the Post-Reconstruction Era: The Rise of Industrial America.* Vol. 6. New York: McGraw-Hill, 1984.

Sullivan, E. Thomas, ed. *The Political Economy of the Sherman Act: The First One Hundred Years.* New York: Oxford University Press, 1991.

Tipple, John. "The Robber Baron in the Gilded Age," in *The Gilded Age,* ed. H. Wayne Morgan. New York: Syracuse University Press, 1970.

Walker, Albert H. *History of the Sherman Law of the United States of America.* New York: Equity Press, 1910.

FURTHER READING

Burgan, Michael. *J. Pierpont Morgan: Industrialist and Financier.* Mankato, Minn.: Coughlan, 2006.

Edge, Laura. *Andrew Carnegie.* Minneapolis, Minn.: Lerner, 2003.

Holly Cefrey. *The Sherman Antitrust Act: Getting Big Business Under Control.* New York: Rosen, 2004.

Parker, Lewis K. *J. Pierpont Morgan and Wall Street.* New York: Rosen, 2003.

———. *John D. Rockefeller and the Oil Industry.* New York: Rosen, 2003.

Segall, Grant. *John D. Rockefeller: Anointed with Oil.* New York: Oxford University Press, 2001.

WEB SITES

"John Pierpont Morgan," Spartacus Educational
http://www.spartacus.schoolnet.co.uk/USAmorgan.htm

"J.P. Morgan," PBS.org
http://www.pbs.org/wgbh/amex/1900/peopleevents/pande10.
html

The Robber Barons
http://history.sandiego.edu/gen/soc/robber-barons.html

"The Sherman Antitrust Act," The Linux Information Project
http://bellevuelinux.org/sherman.html

"The Sherman Antitrust Act of 1890," Civics Online
http://www.civics-online.org/library/formatted/texts/
sherman_antitrust.html

"Short Biography of Andrew Carnegie," BiographyShelf.com

http://www.biographyshelf.com/andrew_carnegie_biography.html

"Short Biography of Thomas Edison," BiographyShelf.com

http://www.biographyshelf.com/thomas_edison_biography.html

"Were the founders of American industry 'robber barons' or 'captains of industry'?" The Social Studies Help Center

http://www.socialstudieshelp.com/Lesson_44_Notes.htm

PHOTO CREDITS

PAGE

3: Library of Congress, cph 3c16287

6: The Pierpont Morgan Library/Art Resource, NY

10: Library of Congress, cph 3b32519

14: The New York Public Library/Art Resource, NY

17: Library of Congress, ppmsca 17523

25: The Francis Firth Collection/Art Resource, NY

28: Snark/Art Resource, NY

42: Art Resource

46: AP Images, NYC Transit Authority

50: Library of Congress, ggbain 03804

52: Library of Congress, cph 3a04860

67: Library of Congress, cph 3c20765

74: The Granger Collection, New York

79: Library of Congress, cph 3b10756

85: Library of Congress, cwpbh 04451

94: Getty Images

98: The New York Public Library/Art Resource, NY

INDEX

advertising, 44
agriculture, 18, 21–22, 26–32
Aluminum Company of
  America, 103
American Federation of Labor
  (AFL), 66
American Hoop, 5
American Revolution, 20–22
American Steel and Wire
  Company, 5, 8
American System, 27
American Telephone and
  Telegraph (AT&T), 64, 103
American Tin Plate Company, 5
American Tobacco Company,
  45, 101
Anti-Monopoly Party, 68–69
Articles of Confederation,
  15–16

Bacon, Robert, 8
Baltimore and Ohio Railroad, 24
Bank of the United States,
  17–18, 33, 37
bankruptcy laws, 56
Bell, Alexander Graham, 44
bonds, 62–63
boycotts, 19–20
bribery, 51
Brown, Moses, 30–31
Bryan, William Jennings, 61
Buchanan, James, 54–55
Bureau of Corporations, 101
business laws, 32–33, 89
Butler, Benjamin, 68–69

Calhoun, John C., 35–36
cameras, 44
canals, 24, 34–35

Carnegie, Andrew
  financing of new industries
    and, 64
  innovation in steel industry
    and, 41
  J.P. Morgan and, 1, 7–11, 97
  Morrill Tariff and, 55
  trusts and, 5–7
  wealth of, 68
Carnegie Steel, 1, 4–7
Charleston and Hamburg
  Railroad, 24
Chicago, Burlington & Quincy
  Railroad, 64, 99
cigarettes, 44–45
Clay, Henry, 35–36
Clayton Antitrust Act, 102, 104
Cleveland, Grover, 69, 93
coal, 41–42, 43
colonies, 12–15, 54–55
competition, 57–59, 63–64
consolidation, 58–59
corporate mergers, 61, 92
corruption, 69
cotton industry, 28–29, 31, 69
craftsmen, 13
credit, 36
Crime of '73, 82
currency, 81–82
Czolgosz, Leon, 95

damages, 88, 89
*Dartmouth College v.
  Woodward*, 33
Department of Commerce and
  Labor, 101
distilling industry, 14
dividends, 7
Dodd, Samuel C.T., 60–61

Drew, Daniel, 49–51
Drexel, Anthony, 62
Duke, James Buchanan, 44–45
DuPont Corporation, 101

Eastman, George, 44
E.C. Knight Company, U.S. v., 90
economy, 12–15, 52–53, 68–73
Edison, Thomas, 44, 45–47, 51
electricity, 41
Elkins Act, 101
Embargo Act, 19–20
embezzlement, 49
eminent domain, 33
enforcement, 74–76, 79
Erie Canal, 34–35
Erie Railway, 49–51
Evans, Oliver, 26

factories, earliest, 27–32
federal government, state debts
    and, 16–17
Federal Trade Commission
    (FTC), 102–103, 104
Federalist Party, 34
firearms, 29
Fisk, Jim, 49–51
Fitch, John, 26
Fourteenth Amendment, 56
Fulton, Robert, 26, 32, 35

Gary, Elbert, 7
Gates, John Warne, 8
General Electric Company, 47, 64
George, Henry, 70
George, Zachariah, 86
Gibbons v. Ogden, 33
gold, 40, 62, 81–82
Gould, Jay, 49–51
Granger Cases, 73–76
grassroots movement, 65–68
Great Northern Railroad, 64, 99
Green, Hetty, 96
gross domestic product, 39

Hamilton, Alexander, 16–18
Harriman, Edward H., 64
Harrison, Benjamin, 69, 88, 93
Hart-Scoss-Rodino Antitrust
    Improvement Act, 103
Hayes, John, 66
Hayes, Rutherford B., 80
Hepburn Act, 102
Hill, James J., 63–64
Hoar, George, 87, 89–90

Illinois, Munn v., 73
implied power, 18
imports, boycotts on, 19–20
incentives, manufacturing
    and, 18
Industrial Revolution, 22
industrialization, 18, 27–32,
    38–40
interchangeable parts, 29
interlocking directorates, 104
International Harvester, 64
Interstate Commerce Act, 58, 71,
    73–76
Interstate Commerce
    Commission (ICC), 74–76, 101
invisible hand, 52–53

Jackson, Andrew, 22, 25–26, 55
Jamestown, 54
Jefferson, Thomas, 19–20
J.P. Morgan & Company, 62–64

Kansas-Nebraska Act, 80
kerosene, 43
kickbacks, 73
Knight Company, U.S. v., 90
Knights of Labor, 66
Knox, Philander C., 99–100

laissez-faire government,
    52–53, 54
Lancaster Pike, 24
land ownership, 53, 70–71

Legal Tender Act, 81
legislation, 53
liability, 33
light bulbs, 47
limited liability, 56
Lloyd, Henry Demarest, 71
loans, 53
Louisiana Purchase, 80
lumber industry, 47

Madison, James, 20
manufacturing, national support
  of, 19
Marshall, John, 33
Maryland, McCulloch v., 33
McCormick Harvester Works, 64
McCulloch v. Maryland, 33
McKinley, William, 80, 82, 92, 95
mergers, 61, 92
Microsoft Corporation, 103
middle class, 68
mining, 40–41
modernization, 39–40
Mohawk and Hudson
  Railroad, 24
monopolies, 33, 88–90
Monroe, James, 35–37
Morgan, John Pierpont
  antitrust suits against,
    99–100
  competition and, 57
  electric companies and, 47
  overview of, 61–64
  United States Steel and, 2–4,
    8–11
  wealth of, 97
Morgan, Junius Spencer, 61–62
Morrill Tariff, 55
Morse, Samuel F.B., 26
muckraking, 71
Munn v. Illinois, 73

national banks, 17–18, 33, 37
National Biscuit Company, 92

National Tube, 5, 7
nationalism, 16
negligence, 33
New York Central Railroad, 51,
  58–59, 63
Newbold, Charles, 29–30
newspapers, 43–44
Non-importation Act, 19
Nonintercourse Act, 20
Northern Pacific Railroad, 64, 99
Northern Securities Company,
  99–100

Ogden, Gibbons v., 33
oil, 42–43, 59–61

Pan-American Exposition, 95
patents, 43
Pennsylvania Railroad, 63
People's Party, 69
photography, 44
plows, 29–30
pooling arrangements, 5, 58
poverty, 66–68, 70–71
practical adding machines, 43
printing process, 43–44
private enterprise, 18
private ownership, eminent
  domain and, 33
Progress and Poverty (George), 70
Progressive Party, 69
protective tariffs, 15, 18, 36,
  54–55, 81
punishments, 87, 88, 89

railroads, 24–26, 33, 39
  antitrust suits against, 99–100,
    101–102
  competition and, 57–58
  cooling and, 44
  court decisions and, 73–76
  grassroots movements and,
    66, 72–73
  Jay Gould and, 49

J.P. Morgan and, 62–63
limited liability and, 56
raw materials, 18, 40–43
Reagan Amendment, 87
rebates, 73, 101
rebuilding, 20–22
Republican Party, 34–36, 69
restraint of trade, 69, 104
Resumption Act, 81
roads, 24
Rockefeller, John D., 43, 53,
   59–61, 92, 96–97
Roosevelt, Theodore, 95–104
rule of reason, 102–103

*Santa Clara County v. The
   Southern Pacific Railroad*, 56
Schwab, Charles, 1–4, 7–9
Second Bank of the United
   States, 37
Sherman, John, 80–82, 83–86
Sherman, William Tecumseh, 80
Sherman Silver Purchase Act, 82
shipping. *See also* Canals
   boycotts and, 19–20
   colonial economies and, 13
   government support of,
      35–36
   seizures and, 19
silver, 40, 82
Slater, Samuel, 27, 30–31
slavery, 80
Smith, Adam, 52–53
Southern Pacific Railroad, 56, 64
*Southern Pacific Railroad, Santa
   Clara County v.*, 56
Standard Oil Company, 59–60,
   71, 101
state debts, federal government
   and, 16–17
steamboats, 26, 32, 34–35
steel, 5, 41, 55. *See also* Carnegie
   Steel
Stewart, William, 86–87

stocks, 51, 61, 62–63
"Story of a Great Monopoly,
   The" (Lloyd), 71
sugar trust, 69
supply and demand, 32–33, 53
Swift, Gustavus, 44

Taft, William Howard, 102–104
tariffs, protective, 15, 18, 36,
   54–55, 81
taxes, 33
telephones, 47
Tennessee Coal and Iron
   Company, 103–104
Texas, antitrust act of, 78–79
textile mills, 26, 30–31
transportation, 23–26, 43–44. *See
   also* Railroads
trusts, overview of, 4–5
Turpie, David, 86
typewriters, 43

Union Pacific Railroad, 64
United States Steel, 10–11, 64,
   103–104
U.S. v. E.C. Knight Company, 90

Vanderbilt, Cornelius, 51, 58–59
vertical integration, 4
voting trusts, 61

Washington, George, 16, 25
watered stock, 49, 51
Wealth Against Commonwealth
   (Lloyd), 71
Wealth of Nations, The (Smith),
   52–53
Westinghouse, George, 43
whiskey trust, 69
Whitney, Eli, 28–29
Wilson, Woodrow, 104
Wood, Jethro, 29–30
*Woodward, Dartmouth College
   v.*, 33

ABOUT THE AUTHOR

TIM MCNEESE is associate professor of history at York College in York, Nebraska, where he is in his seventeenth year of college instruction. Professor McNeese earned an associate of arts degree from York College, a bachelor of arts in history and political science from Harding University, and a master of arts in history from Missouri State University. A prolific author of books for elementary, middle and high school, and college readers, McNeese has published more than 90 books and educational materials over the past 20 years, on everything from the founding of Jamestown to Spanish painters. His writing has earned him a citation in the library reference work, *Contemporary Authors*. In 2006, Tim appeared on the History Channel program, *Risk Takers, History Makers: John Wesley Powell and the Grand Canyon*. He was a faculty member at the 2006 Tony Hillerman Writers Conference in Albuquerque, where he lectured on American Indians of the Southwest. His wife, Beverly, is an assistant professor of English at York College. They have two married children, Noah and Summer, and three grandchildren, Ethan, Adrianna, and Finn William. Tim and Bev sponsored study trips for college students on the Lewis and Clark Trail in 2003 and 2005 and to the American Southwest in 2008. You may contact Professor McNeese at tdmcneese@york.edu.